You've Been Framed

You've Been Framed

How to Reframe Your Wealth
Management Business and Renew
Client Relationships

Ray Sclafani

WILEY

For general information on our other products and services or for technical
support, please contact our Customer Care Department within the United
States at (800) 762–2974, outside the United States at (317) 572–3993 or fax
(317) 572–4002.

Wiley publishes in a variety of print and electronic formats and by print-on-
demand. Some material included with standard print versions of this book
may not be included in e-books or in print-on-demand. If this book refers to
media such as a CD or DVD that is not included in the version you purchased,
you may download this material at http://booksupport.wiley.com. For more
information about Wiley products, visit www.wiley.com.

ISBN: 978–1–119–06201–1 (Hardcover)
ISBN: 978–1–119–07987–3 (ePDF)
ISBN: 978–1–119–07957–6 (ePub)

Printed in the United States of America
10 9 8 7 6 5 4 3 2 1

To my beloved wife, life-learning partner, best friend, and soul mate. Sally, I love you with all of my heart! Your unending love and support has provided me the confidence to dream big for us. It's corny, it's true: You complete me. Cent'anni, BAV! Love, Harry!

To our boys, Jonathan and Nicholas. You both inspire me, each day, to become the most I can be. You are God's greatest blessings that Mom and I could ever have hoped for. May you both soar to heights far above what we could have ever dreamed. I only hope this work is an example of possibility for you. Remember to laugh and play along the way!

To my mom, who showed me the way—who has been and I know will always be there for me. I love you.

To Nana, who sent me that $25 in college and helped feed me when I had nothing. I love you. Happy 93 years young!

To my clients, current and past, who have trusted in me, partnered, and been willing to give me a chance. Thank you, from the bottom of my heart, for believing in our work together.

To every great financial advisor across the globe. Your work inspires me. May you continue to positively impact the lives of your clients and change the world for the better in the noble work you do each and every day. Thank you for your unending commitment to excellence.

Contents

Foreword

When I first met Ray Sclafani in the early part of this century, he was leading the wholesaling team for Alliance Bernstein's mutual funds. He struck me as an earnest, caring, driven executive who was confident in his abilities but not naïve enough to think he had all the tools necessary to be truly great. In other words, he was a perfect student.

Since then, I have had hundreds of interactions with Ray both personally and in combination with the clients he has served. I was there in the beginning as he started to frame out his business structure for his new business, ClientWise. Since then, he has helped hundreds of financial professionals transform the way they organize their practices and consciously execute a plan.

I was struck by his willingness to hear feedback with an open attitude and his commitment to making decisions based on these ideas. I found him to be one of the hardest-working people in this business, who never settled for mediocrity and who never tolerated being average. Interestingly, this is the basic tenet of his book, *You've Been Framed*.

Ray is able to draw on his many years in business development, management, and ownership to craft a compelling narrative for entrepreneurs seeking to get to a new level of fulfillment with their firms. I found his modular approach to helping advisors evaluate, address, and resolve challenges to be especially thoughtful. It allows readers to contemplate a question, then refer back to the relevant sections of the book to process the optimal outcome.

The financial services profession is going through a profound change. What has worked in the past will not work in the future. Today's economics, demographics, and regulatory environment introduce a whole new set of challenges for the business. In my experience, I find the profession divided into two camps: those who live in the past and complain about the present and those who see the present as a catalyst for the future.

What Ray has done with this book is give structure to those who wish to transform their business from a vehicle for generating income to one that makes an impact on the lives of others. It is an important addition to your business book library.

Mark C. Tibergien

Acknowledgments

It was in the spring of 2003, as I recall, that Dan Sullivan of Strategic Coach suggested to me that I consider building my own firm. Soon thereafter, he challenged me to write a book. Well, years later, I decided for myself that it was time. Thanks, Dan . . . for the freedom, the fun, and the challenge to think creatively, follow my unique ability, and make every day a positive focus. You helped me make this work possible.

There are many friends, colleagues, and neighbors who helped shape me as a human and as a professional.

Joan Weltz, may God rest her soul, taught me in the fourth and fifth grade at P.S. 79 in Whitestone, Queens, that it was okay to try new things and that even if I wasn't great at something, I could learn and take risks. She gave me the confidence to know, even at a young age, that it was the adventures in life that brought great surprises—and that a move to Texas was BIG!

It was Mr. Bennett of J. J. Pearce High School who had such vision and figured out how to mobilize so many high school kids to show up at 0-dark-thirty—to shoe-polish marks on the parking lot to teach us how to march our way right onto that football field every Friday night and believe. He was also the guy who told me I couldn't be the leader of the band. Whew! That was important.

Also to be remembered are the many professors at Baylor University who took such great care to make sure I made it, who supported me, who taught me lots of life lessons, and who helped make me into who I am today.

Then there was the one trip, and the only trip, where I would learn from my Uncle Len how to commute, at 17, from Bayside by bus, the Q16, to Flushing for the 7 train to Grand Central, where I would change to the 4 or 5 downtown to Wall Street, before walking up Broadway to 140. During that trip, it was Uncle Len who taught me how to fold (back in those days) a *Wall Street Journal*, which one must read each and every morning. Thanks for the tokens, Uncle Len! And yes, I did mix the tokens up a bit!

I gratefully acknowledge, too, my former colleagues at Alliance Capital, who just seemed to know exactly where to place me so that I could achieve great results, each and every time: Alan Halfenger, who took a young 17-year-old, gave him a job, and told him just what to do to succeed, and Willie Mae, who ran that mailroom and taught me the importance of locking the safe. It was Jim Yockey who took a chance on me and taught me about the advisor, about learning what was important to helping each advisor build a business, about building the database, and about running a business. But there are so many others who came after Jim, especially Bob Errico, to whom I owe a career. Although Bob may never know how much that visit to Texas meant, while having that lunch at The Palm, it was a full life lesson that would provide career guidance for the many years to come. John, Rick, Mike, Dave, and all of the others! What a ride! Thanks for the memories, the lessons, and the lifetime of friendship. And for all of those great runs through the Park and around the city! Every morning was an individual lesson in what matters.

I send a huge thank you to Bob Powers, who rests in peace; whose wisdom, stories, and catchphrases are priceless, each and every morning, then and now; and who kept me going and thinking and becoming. So, "send in the clowns . . ."

Dr. Marvin Sadovsky, who taught me about communication, partnering, and the belief systems in neurolinguistics, helped me to create this work. That outcome frame is all I ever needed. Thanks for that!

Mr. Carrol Meredith, who also rests in peace, and who spent hours teaching me about this business, was always there for me. His commitment to Merrill Lynch, to his advisors, and to his clients was awe inspiring. Carrol represented all that there was in the phrase, "Do right by others."

My favorite running partner and Jewish father, Harold Rubin, who has been so willing to share his wisdom about life, about work, and about this business, has helped me shape my thinking about the future of financial services.

Thank you to our total team at ClientWise, which has provided such a powerful platform of possibility, for future growth, for our clients, and for ourselves to partner and achieve the unimaginable.

Sophia Harbas, our director of coaching services at ClientWise, has been with me every single professional step of the way, a best friend for Beth and me, and a thinking partner who always knows how to think out of the box. Thanks for being you . . . for leading and for inspiring me to press forward and do our best for others. Your unselfish acts of kindness and partnership are an example for us all. Thanks for the journey. The best is indeed yet to come!

Thank you to Lisa Hanna, our chief of staff, who more than nine years ago signed up for more than I think we both could think of at the time. I'm still amazed at how she keeps the trains running on schedule and fits it all in!

Thank you, Beth Holly. Your attention to detail and project management has truly made this work come together. Thank you very much, Christina. Or is it Kristina?

Last but not least, thank you to Mark Tibergien, for whose knowledge about this industry and vision for where we should come together to think about the future we all owe a great deal. His contributions and dedication that have helped so many others, his intellect and passion, mean more to me than those of any other professional I have ever met. Thank you, Mark!

Introduction

This book is built on the following premise: *Financial advising is a noble profession.* As a financial industry veteran of more than 25 years, I have been witness to the amazing work that advisors do every day to help other people live satisfying, fulfilling, and successful lives.

Financial professionals do meaningful work. They help their clients to design the lives they want to lead and then help them live to the fullest, whether by guiding clients through the challenges of transitioning toward retirement, preparing for and selling a family-owned business when there is no next generation to take it over, making adjustments to original plans because of a divorce, or sending a child to the college of his or her choice. Financial professionals provide support to clients taking care of unexpected health care costs with aging parents and are there as clients work through the financial and maybe even emotional implications of a spouse's death. The most effective financial advisors also speak to their clients about philanthropic giving, endowment work, and setting up trusts, helping to create a positive influence that radiates out into society.

I call it impact work. Why? Because when advisors do their jobs well, not only does their work impact this generation, but it also carries forward through multiple generations. If a financial advisor does a great job with his or her client, that client's children and grandchildren will be better off because of that partnership, as will the charities and endowments to which the client contributes. Society will be better off, too, as advisors have helped clients maximize both their wealth and their ability to pay that wealth forward.

Advisors themselves have an opportunity to create change by the way in which they conduct their practices. As Dan Sullivan puts it, financial advisors of the future will have the opportunity to "innovate more and more fundamental solutions to economic, political, and

1

KEY CONCEPT

Financial advising done at its best is impact work that allows the advisor to make a positive difference in the life of the client, in the lives of the client's heirs, and in all of the diverse parts of society that that client's life touches.

social issues."[1] I am reminded of one advisor client of my firm who has found a way to start schools in Africa for girls and another who is involved in an annual bicycle giveaway to underprivileged children. Sullivan points to the example of an advisor who created a divorce mediation program that could be used not only in financial services but also in legal and counseling services. Whether on a small, medium, or big scale, that's true impact. It's what our profession looks like at its best and what it can be more and more as we move into the future.

GOOD VERSUS EVIL IN THE FINANCIAL INDUSTRY

The idea of the financial profession being noble sounds a lot like heresy if we rely only on what we see in the media. There, we don't hear about the positive side of the financial industry; we hear instead about financial traders under criminal investigation, brokerage firms facing fines, scammers using Ponzi schemes to cheat investors, and decent Americans having their homes foreclosed on due to a mortgage industry gone awry. We see the rawest side of the financial industry depicted in films that showcase sex, drugs, and corruption (*The Wolf of Wall Street* comes to mind); we may witness our neighbors shaking their heads at the mention of the latest financial scandal among the big banks on the evening news or their social-media feed; and we may hear our friends and family complaining about the greed associated with the industry.

In reality, these portrayals represent only a small segment of the financial profession, and they certainly don't represent the typical financial advisor. If you are a financial advisor, you know as I do that the majority of individuals in our industry are principled, hardworking, and committed to serving others. They are taking client calls the night before a holiday because they want to make sure their clients get the service they deserve. They are reading up on the tax code on weekends to make sure they have the latest information for their clients long before April 15 rolls around. They update their knowledge of the capital markets frequently. They are curious about people, and they are excellent listeners. They are dedicated to their clients' financial health and prosperity, and they are not counting their paychecks as the media sometimes suggests.

While it's true that being a financial advisor and being the founder of a financial advisory firm have monetary benefits, the majority of the financial professionals with whom I have had the honor of serving and partnering are empathic, notable for their deep integrity, and committed to serving others. Throughout this book, you will read many of their stories, which reveal the approach they are taking to help accelerate their own success and how they partner with clients. I have the unique good fortune of occupying a front-row seat to observe the work of the best in the business, and I will share what I've learned with you.

KEY CONCEPT

Despite media coverage of negative and scandalous financial industry stories, financial advisors are, by a wide margin, hardworking, principled, knowledgeable, and generous individuals who are a credit to the industry and to their clients.

WHO THIS BOOK IS FOR

As you decide whether to purchase this book or whether to read deeper, you may be wondering whether this book is for you, given that there are so many different types of financial professionals out there. In fact, this book is for financial advisors of any type—wirehouse, independent broker-dealer, and registered investment advisors—who are interested in enriching and/or expanding their teams, strengthening their client relationships, and growing their practices.

In particular, if you are an advisor who knows you have something valuable to offer your clients but you are asking yourself whether you and your firm are doing an effective job of communicating that value,

this book is for you. If you are a financial advisor who has found yourself thinking about your professional brand lately and wondering if it is
developed enough to attract your ideal client, this book is also for you.
Maybe you have yet to define your own brand or specific value proposition, but you do know that you'd like to grow your practice, and you
recognize that there is room for you to do a better job of marketing
your services. Or perhaps you've been pigeonholed by some of your
clients: They don't understand the full breadth of services you offer,
and you're ready to break out of that narrow mold and create a brand
that is as big as you now are. If so, this book is for you.

This book is also for those advisors who want to be able to sell their
firm someday and who are seriously thinking about an exit strategy.
This book will help these advisors clarify their value proposition to
clients and learn to document that value, so others on the team can
replicate the unique capabilities and approach of their firm and scale
them over time for greater profit.

Last, this book is for those advisors who believe in the potential of
this profession to help people live better lives and who are interested
in having a positive impact on others and leaving a legacy.

Come Together: Calling Advisors from Every Channel

We have all heard the debates regarding which channel serves clients
the best. We have witnessed regulations being created to designate
which advisors can claim that they have a fiduciary relationship with
their clients. And we have seen the rivalry that can occur between
professionals in competing channels. We will not engage in that debate
here. In fact, we will proceed under the premise that every channel has
its value and that we all have something to learn from one another.

Regardless of the channel in which an advisor chooses to operate—
wirehouse, independent broker-dealer, hybrid, insurance, or registered
investment advisor, to name a few—almost all financial advisors are
working diligently to provide the very best they can for their clients.
These advisors are committed to doing well by their clients, regardless
of any public suspicion that it's all about making money for themselves.

There are debates about whether the wirehouse folks have allegiance to their clients versus their corporations, for example, but I invite you to set those debates aside for now and focus instead on the reality that all financial advisors, regardless of channel, are in this together.

Even with the differences among us, we are all part of the same industry, and it is up to us to set the tone of engagement for the future. Go competitive and go negative and we only feed the public's perception that advisors are focused on profits rather than people. Choose instead to see value in different approaches and to opt for collaboration, and we not only help create a positive face for the public but we also increase the chances of elevating our own industry. If we remain client focused and "client-wise," we can all benefit. In a rising tide, all boats will rise together.

THE GOODS: WHAT THIS BOOK CONTAINS

This book provides all the tools you need to consider how you may wish to reframe yourself, your team, and your firm, as well as to engage in the actual reframe. While the reframe itself ultimately will be unique to your firm and your clients, the process to get there is consistent across firms, as I and my team have tested, refined, and perfected it over the years with thousands of financial advisors. We share it here with you. In fact, I have included in this book everything I believe you will need to successfully reframe your practice. This includes key concepts to help you understand the philosophy behind reframing, assessment tools to help you identify important patterns, coaching questions that enable you to reflect, a step-by-step formula for engaging in the reframe, hands-on exercises to move forward, and industry insight from top financial leaders that will make your reframe even more effective. You will also be given access to online resources and an online community of other financial professionals with whom you can engage, chat, brainstorm, ask questions, and share insight to make sure you don't have to go it alone.

This book is divided into three sections. "Part I: You Gotta Believe" covers the thinking and philosophy behind why the reframe is

Are You Ready?

To successfully engage in the reframing process, you must be willing to hear feedback from others with an attitude of openness, invest the effort to reflect on that feedback, and make a series of important decisions about what you want to really stand for, now and in the future. You must also be ready to do the necessary work in a consistent way if you're going to succeed. This book can serve as a useful tool in the development of your frame and the frames of your firm and your team of professionals. If you are open and engaged in the process, it will work for you.

important. This part will help you create new thinking patterns that can inspire and motivate you to engage in the hard work of reframing your practice. You have to be open to the possibility of some shifts in your thinking and beliefs before you can engage in the reframing process. You may also find out while reading this first part of the book that you're on the right track and/or that how you're currently framed is exactly how you wish to be framed. That can help increase the confidence of all members of your team, including you as the leader, while keeping you all motivated and energized to continue on your path of success and development.

Then, "Part II: Five Steps to Reframing Your Business" gives you a step-by-step plan for how to effectively reframe your practice. This section is full of support tools—coaching questions, checklists, exercises, online resources, and more—to help you create a powerful new frame that will help you meet your goals for your practice. In particular, Part II will help you

- determine how your clients are currently framing you,
- explore what you'd really like to be seen as representing and match this up with your clients' actual needs,
- create a marketing story to communicate your new frame to others,
- reengage your clients with your new story so they can fully partake in your firm's services and tell others about your story, and

■ build a network of trustworthy professionals who will help you deliver on your promise to your clients and spread the word about what you do.

Part II will help you create an authentic marketing approach that builds a bridge between what you want to provide and what your clients need, so you can grow your business in a conscious and purposeful way that meets both criteria. It's the ultimate setup for long-term success, whether that's defined as selling your business someday for the greatest return or watching your firm continue into the next generation.

In "Part III: Now What?" you will learn how to assess whether you have effectively reframed your practice by looking for 10 specific signals. This can be as rewarding as hearing your client tell someone else about your services and nailing them spot on or as simple as discovering that you like to go to work once again. Part III will also review key concepts, talk about the future of advising, and highlight some of the additional free resources awaiting you online as you engage in reframing your business. These resources include helpful checklists, articles, and opportunities to converse with other financial leaders.

JOINING TOGETHER TO CREATE A NOBLE PROFESSION

I sincerely believe that the financial profession is a noble one and that advisors have the potential to make a huge impact on their clients and the world. This book is meant to help advisors reach their full potential so they can not only achieve their own goals as business owners but also benefit their clients, transform the industry, and change the world. Are you ready to join me?

I'm invested in the journey and here's why.

My dedication to the financial industry is rooted in my long history with the profession. I first joined the industry at 17 years of age, when I was fortunate enough to get a job working at 140 Broadway in downtown Manhattan as a summer intern for Alliance Capital, which was really beginning to grow as a mutual fund company. Although I was born in New York, I had moved to Texas at age 11; six years later, I came back to New York to learn the ropes in financial services. I ended up earning enough summer money at Alliance Capital to put myself through my first year of college at Baylor University.

At Baylor, I learned a lot about myself, a lot about values, and a lot about integrity. I owe a great deal to the university and to the many professors there who invested in helping to shape who I am today. I was taught at Baylor that we get to grow up to be whatever we wish to be, to be curious and learn from others, and to be a journey learner. I remember, too, one of my professors reminding me upon graduation that the journey for learning had only just begun.

For 20 years, I chose to work in the asset management space for Alliance Capital, which became Alliance Bernstein, in multiple capacities. I started in operations when I was 17, where I learned the business from the inside out; next, I moved into an inside sales role and then a field sales professional role, meeting with financial advisors, which I did for more than a decade. Then I was recruited to be part of the leadership team, where I was responsible for leading the bank channel, the independent financial planning channel, the registered investment advisor channel, and the insurance channel. It was a long, prosperous, and wonderful career that gave me an opportunity to understand the financial industry in a way that an outsider cannot.

I had always felt called to make a difference in the lives of others, so I decided to engage in that calling more fully: I left Alliance Bernstein and trained to become a professional certified coach. By January 2006, I had launched ClientWise, dedicated to coaching the financial professionals with whom I'd worked for so long. In this work, I have the pleasure of leading a team of coaches who help many top professional advisors discover how their clients view them and discern how they would like their clients to view them in the future. These coaches also work with advisors as they rebuild their frames and grow their referral networks to create businesses with greater value, purpose, and longevity.

In addition to leading a team of more than 25 coaches and growing ClientWise, I have the pleasure of traveling the United States and internationally to speak to, train, and coach top-tier financial professionals. I continue to discover that as highly capable as advisors are, there are still discrepancies—sometimes big, sometimes small— between how they see themselves and how others see them, clients and team members included. That is why I have written this book. It excites me to be an advocate for financial advisors and for the great work many of them do for others. I think that if advisors listen to clients, connect to their own passions, and match the two, their work can truly change the world.

I bring a unique background to my current work as an executive coach and CEO of a coaching company dedicated to financial professionals. While other coaches in this space may have covered the financial industry as journalists or have come out of a more general business background, I have worked directly in the financial industry for more than two decades, rising through the ranks and learning how the business operates, from rainmaking and relationship development to team building and practice management.

I also have a personal familiarity with the process of reframing, having done it many times over the years: as a Texan working in New York City, a New Yorker working in Texas, a salesman who became a leader, a field sales guy who moved to the home office, a wholesaler that grew to be a national sales director, and a financial services leader who became an executive coach to financial leaders.

Ultimately, my intention in writing this book is to make a positive difference in the lives of others, from the financial professionals who read this book to the clients they serve, who will be affected for the better. But it's a journey that we have to take together. If we are going to evolve the industry and pull so many clients up with us, we must agree to listen to our clients, try new pathways, work hard, and go back again to our clients to listen to their feedback until we get things right. In the process, we can fall back in love with the profession and spend our time doing more of what we love.

Are you out, or are you in?

Harold Rubin, a good friend of mine who is also a mentor, will often remind me that my job is to grow into the most that I can be each and every day. "Yesterday is over," Harold will say. "What do you plan to do today to become the most that you can be?" I would like to challenge you to ask yourself this same question. By engaging in the reframe process, you will have the capability to ask and answer, "How can we be the best we can be today and in the future for our clients and ourselves?"

HOW TO READ THIS BOOK

While this book can be read from start to finish, you don't have to read the chapters in a particular order or even read the book cover to cover. Feel free to focus on those chapters that most excite you and resonate with you or to view a snapshot of each chapter by reading the key concepts, coaching questions, and industry-insight examples in each. Be sure not to miss the alerts, too, for the complimentary online tools that are available to you on the ClientWise eXchange™ (youvebeenframed.clientwise.com). These unique tools and resources can help you and your team to reframe yourselves, achieve the goals you have set, and ultimately make the kind of difference in the lives of others you hope to make. Icons are used throughout the book to signal each of these different elements.

🔑 Key Concept

⚙️ Coaching Corner

💡 Industry Insight

❌ The eXchange™

The eXchange™ is a first-of-its-kind platform that provides financial advisors with access to proprietary content developed by my company, ClientWise, since 2006 while working with top performers in the industry. As a reader, you will have access to a special book-related set of tools on the eXchange™, as well as to other financial professionals who have read this book.[2] The eXchange™ also provides access to a network of high-performing financial professionals across the nation and the ability to engage with the world's highest-credentialed executive coaches. The membership on the eXchange™ continues to grow; I invite you to take advantage of this opportunity to join.

CONCLUSION

In an industry marked by constant change, the ability to reframe oneself, one's team, and one's practice is essential. Fiduciary standards will continue to evolve, compensation will continue to change, and new technology will continue to emerge, regularly disrupting both the way we do business and the type of service that clients expect and the government demands. Today, it is the robo-advisor; tomorrow, it will be something else, and we can only predict so much.

The ability to reframe your practice will give you the agility you require to stay relevant in tomorrow's world. It will provide you with the tools you need to articulate your value to the client when competing technologies emerge, downward pressure on compensation continues, and the unforeseen changes of tomorrow take place. The ability to reframe will ensure you are ready for that change and that you will be able to evolve again and again over time as the marketplace shifts into its next iteration. Reframing ensures relevance!

NOTES

1. Dan Sullivan, "The Twelve Predictions: Excerpted from *Creative Destruction*, Module 1" (Toronto, Canada: The Strategic Coach, 2007), 3, www.strategiccoach.com/downloads/prb_12Predictions.pdf.
2. The eXchange™ can be found at youvebeenframed.clientwise.com.

PART I

You Gotta Believe

CHAPTER 1

You've Been Framed!

I am willing to bet that as a financial services professional, you show up every day and work hard for your clients. You make phone calls, have in-person meetings, and do quarterly and annual reviews. You crunch numbers when required; you get in your car or on the plane when you need to be somewhere important for your clients; and you do your homework, reading the financial papers, the tax code, and new industry regulations. You tell your team, if you have one, what to do and how to operate to ensure success for the client and the firm. You're working hard and doing everything right. Or are you?

That is the question. As much as work and life are busy, and as easy as it would be to give a quick nod of a yes, if you are really and truly honest with yourself as a financial services professional, the answer has to be "maybe," because you can't really know how you are doing until you take the time to assess.

Have you asked yourself lately how you are doing with your financial services business? Not just in terms of top-line and bottom-line numbers, but in terms of everything that leads to a truly successful career, business, and client community? Here are some questions to consider as you contemplate how successful you really are today.

- Do you have a clear understanding of your firm's unique value, and have you documented that value for yourself and your clients, so that the business not only thrives but also can be replicated, scaled, and sold if desired?

- Are you providing your clients with the comprehensive wealth management services they deserve, or do you just focus on those products and services that you can and care to offer? If you don't offer them, are you willing and able to connect your clients to other respected professionals?

- Have you learned to truly partner with your clients, or are you stuck in the old model of just selling to your clients or telling them what they should do, rather than inviting them to co-create in the process?

- Do you have a team of capable folks who work well together and whom your clients trust, rely on, and value?

- How clear are you about how you charge for your services and the true value that the client finds in what you provide?

- Are you and every member of your team clear about what differentiates you from other financial advisors and the many choices your clients have today?

- How are you working to be relevant in the lives of the heirs of your clients' wealth?

- Do you have the ability to step away from your business to take an extended vacation or a break or, if need be, to deal with a personal or family illness?

- Do you have the desired amount of work–life balance on a day-to-day basis, allowing you to eat right, exercise, spend time with family and friends, and enjoy life however you like to do best?

- Do you have a rock-solid succession plan in place for how your business will continue after you choose to move on to something new or to retire? When put to the test, will that succession plan really work?

These are just some of the questions to explore if you are ready to assess how successful your financial services practice is today—questions that will be explored directly and implicitly in this book.

In the process of asking these questions, you may discover that you are right on track with your business and find greater peace of mind, motivation, and energy in that. Or you may discover it's time for a major reframe. Alternately, you may discover that you simply want to recalibrate your business and your approach to bring greater satisfaction to the work that you do and to your client's satisfaction in the support you provide them.

Whether you simply want to get your numbers up, you have some doubts about where your business is going right now, or you are a lifelong learner, this book has something for you. It will take you on a journey of assessing the state of your financial services practice today, and it will provide you with all the tools you need to reframe for the future if you discover that this is necessary for greater success or more satisfaction.

Like it or not, we've all been framed—whether we've framed ourselves or allowed others to frame us. You are about to become conscious of the way you are framed today—by your team, your clients, the public, and the media—so you can make intentional decisions to ensure that the frame others see you within is the one you meant for them to use. By learning to frame yourself intentionally, you will tap into the fullest degree of your and your firm's potential. Let's look deeper at what it means to be framed.

WHAT'S A FRAME?

The perspective through which people view advisors is the *frame*: the set of beliefs through which others see and define you, your team, and your business. The frame is constructed of those words the client, the media, your team, or anyone else uses to describe what it is that you do and the way in which you do it. The frame may be accurate or it may be false. It may be positive or it may be negative. Do you have a clue how others are framing you?

Wealth management advisor Charles Prothro, CFP, CLU, ChFC, and AEP of Charles Prothro Financial, describes the frame as follows:

"When somebody frames me, they put a wall around me. They put me inside something and they don't necessarily let me out of it—just like a picture frame."[1] Prothro knows all about what it means to be framed, as he was in the life insurance business for 22 years before expanding his business to offer other financial services. "Everyone knew me as a life insurance man. They knew what that meant. They understood that. I would walk into [. . . a client's] life and I was a life insurance policy walking into the room."[2]

Then one day, Prothro gave an insurance check to one of his clients whose husband had just passed away, and a look in her eyes told him that she had no idea what to do with all that money—where to put it or how to invest it. He didn't have a Series 7 license and wasn't in a position to be providing financial advice. Prothro explains, "That's when I walked in the office and told myself, 'I'm never going to have that happen again.'"[3]

Prothro decided then and there to reframe his business to be about more than insurance. He hired an experienced credentialed investment planner and Certified Financial Planner, and he augmented his own credentials to include those of Certified Financial Planner and Chartered Financial Consultant. Prothro also changed his company name from that of his flagship insurance company to Charles Prothro Financial to help him convey the reframe to his clients. Just as important, he made time to educate his clients on the new services he and his team could offer.

Clients responded well to the reframe, with comments like, "Charlie, I'm so glad to know this. I always wanted you to get in this type of business . . . it just adds to the things you're doing for us."[4] Another grateful and appreciative client noted, "Charlie, you treated me the same when I was sending you $50.00 a month for a life insurance policy as you do now with all of our investment dollars."[5] For Prothro, it's all about serving the client fully—and stretching, growing, and reframing to make that happen effectively.

KEY CONCEPT

People tend to view financial advisors through a particular perspective or *frame*. The frame is made up of the set of beliefs through which a person sees, defines, and understands the advisor.

Sometimes the frame gets created by what people see and hear in the media. In the first two decades of the twenty-first century, the media brought to the public news of some nasty events in the financial industry, including the collapse of large banks such as Lehman Brothers, Washington Mutual, and IndyMac; massive illegal-trading discoveries such as the estimated $6.2 billion lost by JPMorgan Chase's "London Whale";[6] and violations of securities laws by supposedly trustworthy banks. Bernie Madoff's Ponzi scheme certainly did damage and left a mark.

After August 2008, hundreds of thousands of Americans watched their investment portfolios and retirement accounts take a nosedive during the Great Recession, while homeowners who were given ill-advised loans struggled to handle mortgage payments. All of these unfortunate issues contributed to a series of potential negative frames that the public sometimes placed on the financial professional.

Not all frames are negative, but this is a helpful place to start because we can see how damaging they can be. Here are some examples of the more negative frames that people may consciously or unconsciously assign to those in the financial services profession:

- Financial advisors are self-serving, greedy, and unprincipled.
- Financial advisors don't really help people; they just sell investments to make themselves richer.
- Most advisors at brokerage houses are just sales automatons peddling the company line.
- My father's financial advisor is old fashioned and I never want to work with him/her.
- My advisor can't do anything for me besides build my retirement portfolio.

Then there are the frames that get placed on advisors due to the way they began their careers. Advisors often admit to me that if they started as insurance sales professionals, they are usually framed as that. If they started as stockbrokers, they are only known as investment advisors. If they started as financial planners selling limited partnerships, they are still viewed by many clients as salespeople. Even after these advisors have expanded, their clients still frame them in old ways that do not acknowledge any growth.

Not every advisor is framed in these ways, nor with every client or prospective client, but certainly these are real frames being used to view some in our industry. Do you want to risk being framed in limiting ways?

INDUSTRY INSIGHT: REFRAMING FOR THE WIN

Erin Botsford, CEO and founder of Botsford Financial Group, understood the value of reframing early in her career. When she first got into the business in the early 1990s, she quickly discovered that clients coming into her office had a "preconceived notion" of her as either a stockbroker or an insurance agent, when in fact she was a certified financial planner.[7]

In addition to being framed with the wrong job description, Botsford also discovered that clients framed her whole profession of financial services as being quite low on the totem pole of professionals and advisors with whom they worked. In Botsford's view, her clients framed their attorneys at the highest level; beneath that, clients put their CPAs and then "probably their Mercedes dealer," she said; financial advisors were situated "way underneath."

Through a blend of mentorship, hard work, recognition of her unique value, and outright brains for the job, Botsford began to reframe herself. She went from being framed as a stockbroker on the bottom rung of the ladder of her clients' trusted advisors to being a savvy and cherished financial advisor who understood estate planning top to bottom. Both clients and other professionals in the field began to turn to her when they needed support in this area. Today, Botsford's firm serves clients in more than 30 states.

Botsford began her early reframe by taking the advice of her mentor, Amy Leavitt, Certified Financial Planner (now of Leavitt Associates), to learn everything she could about estate planning. With Leavitt's support, Botsford identified one of the best estate planning attorneys in the Dallas area and partnered with her to mutually refer clients. But first, Botsford spent a year learning from her new partner how to read and understand estate planning documents, scouring them and learning to point out what was good and bad about them.

Within a year, Botsford became über-skilled at assessing estate planning documents, which allowed her to have brilliant conversations with her clients on the topic—and which won their trust, their business, and their introductions to new future clients. Suddenly, Botsford had a big advantage over her competitors, and high-net-worth clients began seeking out her unique services.

Although there are other important facets to Botsford's growth from solo advisor to CEO of a 15-plus-employee firm, her early reframing efforts had a major positive influence on her success as an advisor and businessperson. Over the years, Botsford has been named one of *Barron's* Top 100 Independent Financial Advisors and Top 100 Women Financial Advisors, one of *D Magazine's* Best Financial Planners, and a *Texas Monthly* Dallas/Fort Worth Five Star Wealth Manager.

Using this book, you can help ensure that your clients see you according to your desired frame, not the frame that they've constructed based on

- negative images from the media,
- their experience working with former advisors, or
- your own ineffective storytelling about your brand!

I know some amazing financial leaders who understand the importance of having a clear brand and who have put generous time and money into the effort, but even the best of the best are sometimes surprised when they explore how their clients perceive them and discover that perceptions don't match up in all areas with their intended brand or frame. This book will give advisors the guidance they need to make a purposeful and effective reframe rather than allowing a de facto, limiting frame to stand unchallenged.

Paul Pagnato, founder and managing director of Pagnato Karp, is very purposeful in how he frames his company. There are three distinct ways in which he works with his team to frame Pagnato Karp: First, they aim to be "recognized as true fiduciaries in the marketplace—[as] a business, a firm and advisors that provide 100 percent pure, objective, transparent advice. That's number one, and very, very important to us." Second, Pagnato works to frame his company as working with the ultra-high-net-worth family and, third, as a family office solution. To implement the frame, Pagnato and team are careful to take a holistic rather than a single-area approach. He believes the latter only leads to frustration and recommends that advisors consider how everything they are doing to frame themselves ties together, whether it's their marketing materials, how their presentation looks, their website, or their print, radio, television, and social media output. Pagnato states, "I believe what has worked for us is looking holistically at all aspects of the marketing, the public relations, the media and branding. It's a comprehensive solution [executed] in a comprehensive way."[8]

KEY CONCEPT

Being aware of your frame is the first step in taking charge of it, by making sure you are defined by your values and work rather than by negative impressions created by scandalous news stories, clients' past experiences with other advisors, or an inaccurate message you are inadvertently sending.

Gabe is an example of an advisor who is stuck in an outmoded frame. He started out 15 years ago selling life insurance and was thought of at the time as a reliable and excellent insurance agent. Fifteen years later, he still has many of the same clients. How do they frame Gabe all these years later? As a reliable and excellent insurance agent. Reliable and excellent are good; unfortunately, the insurance part is flawed because Gabe and his now 10-person firm do more than sell insurance. They also build estate plans, offer beneficiary-designation review, and do tax advising. But most of Gabe's long-term clients don't know about these new services. Gabe never took the time to reframe what he does for his clients, so they have no clue that he provides these other services; he is losing potential business as a result.

Now let's look at a frame that is working effectively for a financial firm. Building Futures Inc. is a firm that offers small to midsize developers and builders lending support, fee analysis, asset protection, and more. Led by their marketing-minded CEO, Miriam, not only has the firm taken the time to get clear on who their audience is and the value Building Futures brings to that audience, but it also regularly communicates its services and value to clients through monthly correspondence and during client check-ins. This firm has taken the steps necessary to create alignment between the value it delivers to clients and what clients perceive it to do. The frame their clients see them through is the one they've carefully and clearly communicated to clients through both service and language. As a result, their clients naturally use that frame to think about and describe the firm, so their firm benefits.

On the one hand, framing is another way to talk about branding and marketing your company—distilling its value and communicating that value with your target market. On the other hand, I would argue that framing, as compared to branding and marketing, more clearly acknowledges the most important element of your success as an advisor: the client! When we talk about branding and marketing, it's easy to fall into the one-sided approach of blaring through a megaphone to the public what services you provide without ever having a dialogue with your target client or stopping to ask, "What does the client, whom my firm is built to serve, actually want and need from my business and our team?"

The process of framing outlined in this book holds the client at the center of the relationship. When you reframe your firm or your team, you will begin and conclude the process by engaging in a series of larger conversations with the client. Provide your clients what they need and your business will grow.

KEY CONCEPT

Reframing begins and ends with the client: what the client needs, what the client believes about you and what you have to offer, and what the client gains in his or her relationship with you as a financial advisor.

THE FIVE LEVELS OF FRAMING

Have you ever met somebody who remembers you from a career 20 years ago and who isn't aware of your career path or how far you've come? And then you reconnect with the person and he or she realizes, "Wow, you've had a lot of different work experiences." It's like the young kid working in an office mailroom who grows up and becomes the CEO of the company but whom people still think of as the young kid in the mailroom. That's framing, and it happens every day.

Framing can happen on multiple levels: at personal, firm, and team levels; among advocates; and within the industry (as shown in Figure 1.1). Personal framing relates to how people view you as an individual person: mailroom clerk versus CEO, nice guy or grouchy

Figure 1.1 The Five Levels of Framing

woman, ambitious employee versus unmotivated worker, reliable individual versus unreliable person, well organized versus disorganized, and so on. Each of these ideas represents a different possible personal frame that you may or may not be pleased with. Soliciting feedback from others is a way to learn more about how they frame you on a personal level.

The firm frame refers to how clients view your practice: its "personality" and values, the kind of clients it works with, the services it provides, and the value it offers to clients. For example, is your firm seen as a team of wealth management partners for the client or as a bunch of sales guys and gals waiting to tell the client about the latest investment opportunity? Do your clients think you only do financial planning, or do they know that you offer other wealth management services as well? The firm frame gets even more complex if you are affiliated with a broker-dealer. Now you have to consider the way your clients may automatically view you based on your association with a given broker-dealer as well as the way you would like them to frame you based on your firm's unique personality, values, and enterprise value.

The team frame refers to how the people on your team view you as a leader. Do they see you as fair or unfair? Stable or erratic? Collaborative or dictatorial? Dedicated or distant? Do they see you as taking company profits without being engaged in the practice, or do they see you as a driver of the practice's success? Although their frames vary, team members see every leader through one kind of frame or another. How does your team frame you?

Advocates frame you, too. Advocates are others who serve as ambassadors for you, your firm, or your team. They believe in you and are willing to promote and refer your services to others. It's important to educate advocates on what your intended frame is so they can help you spread the word and attract the right clients for your business.

The last frame relates to how the public views the entire financial industry. This frame is formed in large part by the media, whether through TV commercials that poke fun at the advisor, scandalous headlines in the newspaper, or unbecoming film productions. Although advisors can't do much to control the industry frame, they can control how they are viewed by their clients, their team, and their advocates by having a well-defined frame that they communicate consistently with clients, potential clients, advocates, and the public.

KEY CONCEPT

Reframing happens at the personal, firm, team, advocate, and industry levels. Being aware of these frames is the first step in taking control of them.

COACHING CORNER

How do you think others are framing you, your team, and your firm? The best way to find out is to ask others, but begin with your own hunch. What answers come to mind?

Reframing: What's the Payoff?

It will take effort for advisors to make a reframe—time and resources to interview clients, to brainstorm the new frame, to incorporate the client services the advisors can provide and the clients desire, to create new marketing collateral, and to communicate the new frame to clients—but there is an attractive payoff:

- Informed clients who actively seek your services
- Increased enterprise value
- More client introductions
- A bigger, healthier practice
- Increased personal wealth through your thriving practice
- Freedom to do what you love within and outside of the firm
- Increased job satisfaction
- More work–life balance
- Chance to leave a legacy
- Opportunity to sell the firm if and when desired
- Opportunity to make a greater impact in clients' lives and the world at large

The reframing process is one of discovery. It involves gathering valuable information from current clients and then going within the team to identify and refine what the firm does well and would like to be doing in the future. The end result is a conscious reframe that allows advisors to build satisfying and saleable practices that have a positive impact and can sustain themselves over time. Success is just a reframe away . . .

CONCLUSION

The truth is that as a financial advisor, you've been framed, like it or not. Perhaps you have framed yourself; perhaps you have allowed others to frame you. Many of the frames will be good; some will be not so good. This book is going to help identify the ways you are currently framed by clients, prospective clients, and other trusted advisors and centers of influence. This book will also help you take a purposeful

KEY CONCEPT

By taking charge of how you are framed, you will be able to provide your best services to the clients whose needs match your skills, maximizing your performance and the clients' outcomes.

approach to reframing the way these others see you so that it matches the firm and professional you are today and plan to be tomorrow.

Why leave the framing to chance when you have the power to build your brand in an intentional way? Only by taking the time to discern your value, match it to the needs of your ideal clients, and learn to tell a story about that value through your marketing communication efforts and client and advocate conversations can you be sure that you are creating the team and practice that you truly want to be. That's what we will do together in this book, which is filled with unique takeaways that can significantly alter your financial practice for the better, tomorrow and well into the future.

We will begin by looking at five of the common reframes that advisors can make if they are ready to operate as the best in the business do.

NOTES

1. Charles Prothro, personal interview, March 23, 2015, transcript, p. 1.
2. Ibid.
3. Ibid. p. 2.
4. Ibid. p. 5.
5. Ibid.
6. Patricia Hurtado, "The London Whale," *Bloomberg QuickTake,* last modified April 23, 2015, accessed May 29, 2015, www.bloombergview.com/quicktake/the-london-whale.
7. Erin Botsford, personal interview, March 10, 2015, transcript, pp. 1–2.
8. Paul Pagnato, personal interview, March 23, 2015, transcript, p. 4.

CHAPTER 2

What the Best in the Business Don't Want You to Know

The Five Wealth Management Reframes

What is it that separates the highest-performing financial advisors from everyone else? Is it the ability to sell big? Is it awesome technical expertise? Is it uncanny insight into markets, or is it super-savvy people skills? All of these traits help the best performers rise to the top, but at the core of these advisors' success is . . .

the ability to innovate.

Top-performing advisors—or those whom I call the "best in the business"—can change on the fly and know how to adjust. They shift, modify, and improve as circumstances and contexts change, and they

29

are improving all the time. These advisors are not afraid to reframe when needed; in fact, they know that they will fall behind, maybe even fail, if they don't.

What the top-performing advisors don't want other advisors to know is that they are successful in the business because they are really good at adjusting. Right? No one wins the game because they insist on sticking with the game plan regardless of what they see happening on the playing field. The only way to win is to adjust, and the best in the business *don't* want you to know that they are masters at adapting to changing circumstances. What's more, they are also really good at empowering those around them—on their teams and in their firms—to adjust, too.

Another way to think of it is as a willingness to reframe. Reframing is really about getting a read on where your clients are today and making adjustments to give them the value they desire and deserve. It's about assessing the characteristics of today's world and refining your business to serve clients in this emerging context.

This business is about change. We've seen more change in the past few years than we've seen in the decade prior. Those who survive and thrive embrace the changes and make the appropriate shifts, adjustments, and reframes required to succeed. Those who produce weaker results keep doing the same things over and over while expecting better results. But as Albert Einstein once said, that kind of behavior is the definition of insanity.

KEY CONCEPT

Circumstances, contexts, the world, your and your clients' situations: They are always changing. To be a successful financial advisor, you need to be able to adjust your plans—or *reframe*—on the fly.

At ClientWise, my executive coaching company for financial leaders, we observe practice management and study leadership every day. We have coached thousands of financial advisors, including those ranked in *Barron's* Top 1,000, and we have studied many financial services firms, small and large. I have spoken to advisors all over the country and the world, including Australia, Canada, Hong Kong, and the United Kingdom, and delivered talks to meetings and conferences at Merrill Lynch, Royal Bank of Canada, Northwestern Mutual, Morgan Stanley,

MetLife, Ameriprise Financial, TIAA-CREF, JPMorgan Chase, Raymond James, Nationwide Financial, the Money Management Institute, and *Barron's*. In collaborating with advisors from these different groups, I have learned about where they have succeeded (versus failed) and why.

In our observations and analyses at ClientWise of the top-performing advisors, we have discovered that those who are most successful have *reframed* themselves for wealth management in the twenty-first century. They have discovered that the old game plan no longer works and have engaged in the following five key reframes. These reframes have given them a distinct competitive advantage over others in the industry, allowing them to grow their practices into the most successful entities that they can be. Table 2.1 presents the five reframes—outlining the shifts from the old frames to the new frames—for effective wealth management practices in the twenty-first century.

In each of these five reframes, there is a pattern of partnership. Advisors can only provide comprehensive wealth management by partnering with others, internally and externally, to augment their own specialties and expertise (Reframe #1). Advisors also interact with clients using a partnering relationship rather than a sales-to-customer relationship (Reframe #2). In addition, advisors partner with team members to ensure the best service and outcomes are provided to clients (Reframe #3). What's more, advisors no longer tell clients what

Table 2.1 Wealth Management Practice Reframes for the Twenty-First Century

	Old Frame		New Frame
Reframe #1	I provide my clients with one particular financial service.	→	I provide my clients with comprehensive wealth management that begins with outcomes-based financial planning.
Reframe #2	I sell to my clients.	→	I partner with my clients.
Reframe #3	I am the best at serving my clients.	→	My team is the best at serving our clients.
Reframe #4	I know what is of value to my clients.	→	My clients and my team work together to define what value our clients need and what value my team can provide.
Reframe #5	I allow clients to rent my services until I choose to stop practicing.	→	I build a legacy business that serves multiple generations to come.

they should value; rather, advisors partner with clients to discover what clients need and value and then improve their own practices to provide that (Reframe #4). Last, advisors build a business that outlasts them by partnering with younger financial advisors whom they mentor and to whom they pass their wisdom (Reframe #5).

Today's high-performing advisors have recognized the cultural shift from hierarchy to equality and from authority to partnership. Whether it's the way the Internet has allowed consumer access to information—leveling the playing field between consumers and the professionals who serve them—or the emergence of the sharing economy where people can bypass traditional corporations and turn directly or near directly to others for a car ride, room stay, or grocery delivery, the world is now flatter than ever.

Translate this phenomenon to the world of financial advising and we start to see a shift from a vertical relationship to a more horizontal one. How does this look in practice? It's the advisor moving from behind the desk to sit beside clients. It's not an approach of, "I have all of the information and you need me." Instead, it's an approach of, "All of the information is in the public domain, and my job is to help you make sense of it and to remove the complexity associated with wealth management."

High-performing advisors have recognized this shift from a hierarchical to a collaborative relationship, and they have made the reframes necessary to build their practices on this premise of partnership: advisor to client, but also advisor to internal and external teams as well.

 KEY CONCEPT

The most successful financial advisors have embraced five key reframes of the client–advisor relationship: Successful advisors provide *comprehensive* wealth management services (rather than a single service), they *partner* with clients (rather than sell to them), they provide the services of a *team* (rather than being the sole advisor), they listen to their clients to determine their *individual values* (rather than assuming that this client's goals are the same as other clients' goals), and they build a business that serves and will be around for *future generations* (rather than existing just for the duration of the advisor's working life).

What Makes You the Best in the Business?

Let's talk about what it means to be "best in the business." At Client-Wise, we define the best in the business as those who

- are clear on their enterprise value
- have pristine client relationships
- track record of stellar regulatory compliance
- operate as part of a team
- have strategic hiring strategies to attract, develop, and retain superior human capital
- have sustainable businesses that can outlive their founder
- have next-generation client coverage
- have high retention scores when clients pass away

Assets under management is one way to judge success, but there are so many other factors by which to gauge success as well, from quality of client relationships and ethical track record to business sustainability.

REFRAME #1: I PROVIDE MY CLIENTS WITH COMPREHENSIVE WEALTH MANAGEMENT THAT BEGINS WITH OUTCOMES-BASED FINANCIAL PLANNING

The first secret of the most successful advisory firms is this: Financial advising is no longer just about offering one particular service such as investment advising, insurance, or financial planning. It's about providing support across all the areas of wealth management that are essential to clients: investing, financial planning, financial management, financial reporting, risk management, family continuity, trusteeship, and/or philanthropy (as illustrated in Figure 2.1).

Admittedly, since 2010 there has been a trend for advisors to move from calling themselves "financial advisors" and "financial consultants" to "wealth management advisors." Yet many have made the switch without actually adjusting or reframing the services they offer. These folks call themselves wealth management advisors, but they still focus solely or mainly on investments or whatever individual service they have traditionally offered.

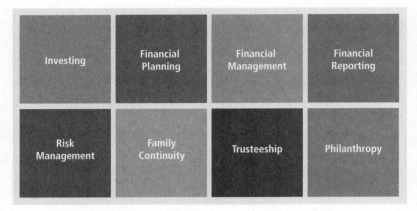

Figure 2.1 Areas of Wealth Management

In contrast, the best in the business understand that this evolution in title goes far beyond semantics. It offers an opportunity for the advisor to go wider and deeper than finances—beyond dollar signs in the bank account and stocks and bonds in the retirement fund—to serve the diverse areas that relate to a client's wealth. Think opportunity! The end result is that these particular firms are able to attract new clients interested in comprehensive support, to capture additional business from existing clients who need and want more, and to increase overall client retention as clients remain satisfied and find value in these firms' offerings.

THE eXchange™
Online Tool 2.1: Your Wealth Management Checklist

How do you define wealth management, and what pieces of wealth management are you best suited to offer? Where do the gaps remain? Building relationships with other select professionals will allow you to do what you love and still support your clients across their wealth management needs. Visit the eXchange™ and complete Your Wealth Management Checklist to focus on which wealth management services your firm would like to offer directly, versus those you can connect your clients to through other professionals on your external team.

At the core of this particular reframe is outcomes-based financial planning to deliver the comprehensive approach of wealth management. We must put financial planning at the core! The financial plan ensures that the advisor and client take everything wealth related into account. For example, there will be no grossly overweighting one stock because you don't realize the client already has investments there, and you won't sell the client life insurance when he or she already has it.

As David B. Armstrong, CFA, president and cofounder of Monument Wealth Management, notes, the financial plan answers the big question of *what is the money for?*[1] As important of a question as that is, plenty of advisors and clients may not have taken the time to answer it. Yet understanding what the money one is making, saving, growing, and managing is for ensures that advisors and clients know how to build the right type of wealth management plan. It also enables them to assess if they are achieving their goals and, if not, to make adjustments along the way.

 COACHING CORNER

The pie of opportunity to service and support clients is big. Which areas of wealth management are you serving? Which ones would you like to serve? Do you have trusted partners and professionals to whom you can refer clients for those areas you don't serve? Reframing your practice will allow you to work through these questions to an end result that helps you grow your business and increase client satisfaction. The hands-on reframing work can be done later in the book, but now is a good time to begin contemplating what kind of wealth management services you currently offer and which ones you may want to expand into in the future.

Where the advisor or firm does not have a skill set, partnerships with other respected professionals can be built. The best of the best do this skillfully. They learn about trusted professionals by going directly to clients to invite them to share their networks, and then they go about building a team of professional advocates that can be used again and again to offer clients a web of support. The advisor stays in the lead, making his or her advice and network indispensable to the client so that others in the network remain partners rather than competitors. A new way of running the wealth management business takes shape, and everyone benefits in the process.

KEY CONCEPT

Moving from calling oneself a financial advisor to embracing the new term *wealth management advisor* should be more than a change in job title. True wealth management involves providing a range of services to help clients achieve their financial goals. If you do not have the specific skill set your client needs, partner with respected professionals who do. Everyone—you, your clients, and your partners—will benefit from the teamwork.

 ### The Benefits of Reframing to Offer Comprehensive Wealth Management

- Clients get their wealth management needs met, meet their financial-related goals, and maximize their wealth and impact on family and community.

- Advisors increase client retention and grow their client base while also creating a strong pipeline of future business through fruitful partnerships with others in the wealth management community.

- Firms have the potential to develop a unique value proposition that renders them ready for a liquidity event down the road.

- Advisors enjoy more meaningful work as they deliver services matched with their own interests while meeting the real needs of their target clients.

- Society benefits as individuals' wealth is maximized and opportunities for philanthropic giving increased.

REFRAME #2: I PARTNER WITH MY CLIENTS

The second reframe of top advisory firms is that they have stopped *selling* to their clients and started *partnering* with their clients. In a sales relationship, the advisor has a series of financial products and/or services that he or she suggests to the client for purchase or investment. In a partnering relationship, instead of suggesting what to buy, the advisor works with the client to formulate wealth goals and to co-create a plan for achieving those goals. Investments may well be made in support of those goals, but it comes out of a partnering rather than a sales relationship.

In a wealth management partnership, it's not about the advisor's agenda, but the client's agenda. As a result, the advisor uses his or her expertise to support the client and the client's goals at the same time that the client is brought more intimately into the relationship to be an active participant in meeting goals and creating financial success.

In the view of Geri Eisenman Pell, CEO of Pell Wealth Partners, it's not that the sales piece is "bad" or has to be removed entirely from the equation, but there is a big difference between being a "product pusher" and someone who offers financial products to clients in service of a well-thought-out financial plan.[2] As Pell puts it, "If you lead with financial planning and if you're always filling a need that a person has and never filling your need to sell a product, then . . . there's no negative connotation to it." Pell understands that the client comes first and has always taken the latter approach. As a result, she explains, "I've never had anybody say to me, 'You're just selling this because it's a product you want to offload.' Never."

The best advisors recognize that the value of the profession is no longer to simply sell to—or even advise or consult with—the client, but instead to create this partnership. They know how to enter into an equal relationship with the client rather than defaulting to the more traditional one-way relationship that has characterized the profession for so long, in which the advisor is the authority and the client is merely the recipient of advice and technical expertise.

The change in the industry from an approach of "sales driven by the advisor" to "partnership driven in service of the client" follows the natural evolution seen in other industries. There we see the relationship between expert and consumer has shifted from a vertical one to a horizontal one as the Internet has given people access to everything, from information to products to services, and has empowered them to step into the role of equal in many areas. In health care, patients now have easy access to online medical advice and their medical records, empowering them to ask doctors more questions and self-report more information to improve their care. In the financial industry, clients can now manage their own portfolios through online accounts, and they have access to the latest financial news, allowing them to be more educated in conversations with their advisors and to make more informed requests.

As clients have become empowered by access to information, they also have developed an expectation that they will be treated as partners in all of their important relationships. They expect their relationship with their financial advisor to be no different. The best in the business recognize this and actively work to create healthy partnerships with clients.

As CEO Pell points out, all too often firms fall into the trap of thinking that investing for their clients and reporting back to them on those investments is enough. In fact, clients need an in-tune, agile advisor who can detect clients' unique financial concerns and respond to them in a satisfactory way. That's partnership.

Pell recounts a telling story on the subject, in which she met an ultra-high-net-worth woman at a charity event who confessed that the brokerage firm that served her and her husband was missing the mark at truly hearing and responding to their concerns.[3]

The husband had some serious financial concerns that were keeping him up at night. Although "the blue shirts" of the firm, as the woman called them, agreed to meet with the couple, the conversation centered around technical jargon that did nothing to put the couple at ease. As a result, the husband continued to suffer from insomnia due to his ineffectively allayed financial concerns. A firm skilled in partnership would have caught their true concerns through active listening and worked through them in dialogue and follow-up action with the clients.

KEY CONCEPT

Rather than selling to the client, your goal should be to partner with the client so that you understand this particular client's needs, which you can then work to meet. Clients are more informed than ever before, thanks to the Internet, so they often already have an idea of where they want to go but need help getting there. Clear communication with your client leads to a stronger relationship, which increases the likelihood of a long-term partnership and successful attainment of financial goals.

Five Steps to an Effective Advisor–Client Partnership

At ClientWise, we encourage advisors to use the following structure to create a healthy partnership. This approach involves more than just an attitude of equality. There are specific actions the advisor engages in to create a successful collaboration.

1. The advisor invites the client to enter into a joint *partnership agreement* that outlines the expectations for the relationship on both sides.

2. The advisor works to *build an effective relationship with the client by fostering trust* and treating the client with respect.

3. The advisor *asks powerful questions* of the client and *actively listens* for answers.

4. The advisor works with the client to *set goals, make plans, and design actions.*

5. The advisor *manages the progress of the client* toward meeting those goals and *provides accountability* for the client regarding follow-through on plans and proposed actions.

It's no mistake that the steps just outlined for creating a healthy wealth management partnership mimic several of the core competencies of the coaching profession.[4] As a coaching firm, ClientWise has intentionally leveraged many of the valuable principles of coaching when training financial leaders on how to create more effective partnerships. It's our goal to share the secrets of coaching with financial advisors, giving them the power to create superb partnerships with their clients. This allows these advisors to move beyond just an attitude of equality to having real tools for building effective partnerships. It also helps them advance beyond their competitors' ability to deliver. In the end, creating a healthy partnership comes from being able to set the foundation for an effective partnership, create a trustworthy relationship, communicate effectively, and facilitate learning and results.

In addition to being what clients *want* today, partnership is also what clients *need* today, and the best advisors are recognizing this. Clients are busier than ever; they are flooded daily with data and communications to process and manage, and the varying elements of their wealth picture have become more complex. Today's client welcomes the support of a wealth management partner who is attentive to the whole wealth picture *and* willing to engage with the client as a collaborator. The best in the business see these opportunities and engage.

REFRAME #3: MY TEAM IS THE BEST AT SERVING OUR CLIENTS

What the best in the business also don't want you to know is that they are not doing it all anymore. They are engaged in the firm but in a different way, using all of their knowledge, wisdom, and experience to *lead a team*, so they are able to truly enjoy the work they do for clients without feeling stretched thin, and so they can deliver on their promise to always be there for the client.

Instead of carrying the mind-set of "I am the best at serving my clients," the best in the business have reframed to "My team is the best at serving our clients." These advisors have broken away from the notion that they have to do it all or that they all have to do it. They are enabling their teams to be the best at serving clients so they don't have to handle the sizable endeavor alone.

The truth is that it's a tough business to work in alone: managing the portfolios, working solo with clients, running the numbers, working to win new clients, and so on. The best in the business, however, get to enjoy using their wisdom to lead a group of people working interdependently to support the client. There is true satisfaction in that. These leaders aren't about doing everything themselves; they are about engaging in a different way that draws on their wisdom and lets them stay involved while retaining the freedom to grow well beyond the early days of their practice, when they were occupied doing everything.

In the old days, many advisors could successfully go it alone. It was hard work, but it was doable. As the financial advising profession has grown more sophisticated, however, the need for a team has increased. Not only has the profession moved from the more narrow financial advising and consulting approach to the more comprehensive wealth management approach with all its growth ramifications, but the work that advisors do within any area of wealth management now has several important pieces to it: technical expertise, client service, client relationship, marketing/acquisitions, and practice management

Figure 2.2 Areas of the Wealth Management Practice

(as illustrated in Figure 2.2). This is in addition to the effort that must now be expended to grow the team of the firm, such as hiring human capital, building company culture and values, managing the team daily, and leading the firm with a long-term strategy in mind.

To expect a single advisor to handle all of these responsibilities is both unrealistic and absurd. The firm suffers, the client suffers, the advisor suffers, or most likely all three do. Building a team takes time, effort, and patience, yes. But the reward in return is freedom for the

KEY CONCEPT

As the number of services wealth management advisors are expected to provide has increased, so too has the need for a team of advisors. A one-person financial advising shop used to be realistic, but now, to provide the diverse range of services, keep up with all of the tasks involved in running and growing a business, and provide the best advising experience for clients, such a setup is not ideal. Share the work and multiply your success!

firm's leader, who now has the space to focus on the parts of the firm that he or she enjoys; in the process, the client gets better service and support.

At ClientWise, we define a *true team* as a group of people who are fully committed to mutually defined and extraordinary success of the group as a unit and who hold themselves mutually accountable for the achievement of that success, as well as the methods by which that success is achieved. Let's break that down a bit. Team is

- a group of people
- committed as a unit to mutually defined success and
- engaged in holding each other accountable.

The best in the business recognize that it's about more than just adding people to the roster or bringing people together; it's about getting the right people onto the bus—people who are engaged in defining success and committed to achieving it. The best in the business also understand the meaning and value of accountability and know how to create a culture in which the team holds one another responsible for taking the steps toward success.

 COACHING CORNER

How does the notion of team fit into your financial services practice today? How might it fit into your practice tomorrow? Where is team already strong in your practice, and where do you feel motivated to make improvements?

REFRAME #4: MY CLIENTS AND MY TEAM WORK TOGETHER TO DEFINE WHAT VALUE OUR CLIENTS NEED AND WHAT VALUE MY TEAM CAN PROVIDE

In the old way of operating, advisors worked under the assumption that they knew best what clients needed. They sought value and tried to deliver it to their clients. Today, the best advisors have reframed this idea. It's no longer a case of the advisor pushing so-called value onto the client, but rather a case of advisors inviting clients into a discussion to define what value they seek. The advisor and the advisor's team can then work together to refine and provide that value, both directly and by making the right professional connections for the client.

Most firms are already providing clients value—value that is desirable, useful, and of interest for the future. Yet clients often don't know what that value really is. How often have you heard a client say, "I didn't know you could help me with life insurance"? Or, "I didn't know you could help me with a mortgage." An advisor may offer 10 services, but the client often only knows of two.

In another example of missed value, the client may realize that she meets with her advisor on a yearly basis without understanding that this meeting is more than a sales opportunity for the advisor to get in front of the client: It is actually an important opportunity to check in on the status of action plans and to recalibrate goals. Advisors provide value to clients, but if the client is too busy or not sufficiently informed to recognize the value, frankly, much of its power gets lost. The best of the best advisors recognize the importance of not only becoming intentional about the kind of wealth management services they offer, but they also realize that they have to continually educate the client on what these services are and how they provide value to the client.

 KEY CONCEPT

Clients cannot take advantage of services you offer that they do not know about or don't realize that they need. Make sure both you and your client understand what value your client needs and what value your team can provide.

At ClientWise, we provide advisors with a specific process for partnering with clients to explore their understanding of a firm's current value proposition. During this process, advisors also engage with clients to gather insight into the value that these clients seek, work with their team to refine the firm's value proposition, and then return to the client to share what the refined offerings now are. This process is at the heart of reframing one's wealth management practice and will be explored in full in Part II of the book.

▼ **Five Steps to Reframing**

1. Collect: Advisors speak to clients to identify where they see value in the firm and where they would like to see more value (we call it the *ClientWise Conversation*™).

2. Define: Advisors clearly and intentionally rebrand/reframe themselves by defining their unique profile of wealth management services in response to the client conversation and advisors' own wishes and interests.

3. Design: Advisors create the marketing materials to communicate that brand/frame to clients, professional advocates, and the public.

4. Inform: Advisors go back to clients and educate them on what wealth management services are offered and the accompanying value of each.

5. Renew: Advisors regularly check in with clients to jointly explore what they have achieved together (since they last met, over the course of the year, and over their life's work together). Over time, the clients should be able to describe this value themselves, and advisors should continue to solicit new feedback.

The insight clients can provide during the partnering process can be an invaluable part of your reframing campaign. After all, what use is a reframe if you're offering services that clients aren't interested in? You can offer the most brilliant products in the world and communicate your new frame to your clients brilliantly, but your efforts will be useless if what you are offering isn't what clients want. Once you've taken your client feedback to the drawing board and revised the value your firm can provide on the basis of what clients are looking for, then you are ready to present your reframed services to your clients.

The reframing process enables the advisor to evoke what it is that clients value most while concurrently reminding clients about all the valuable work the firm has done and continues to do for them. During this process, advisors actively educate clients on the value they bring to clients while putting energy into seeking clients' feedback on value and responding to it.

Top-performing advisors know that they can never take for granted that the client appreciates their value—or even understands what they really do. As a result, these advisors invest time and energy in helping to frame and reframe the very value they provide for clients. This enables clients to understand the full benefits of the wealth management partnership and to increase motivation to stay with a firm over the long term. Clients will be more prepared and inclined to make effective referrals to the firm, too, with the potential to bring in new business and help the firm grow. Not only will clients then understand the firm's value—and thus have the capacity to appreciate it—but they will also have the words to tell others about the firm's value. It's a powerful mix that deepens the potential for a firm's success and longevity.

 COACHING CORNER

What value does your firm currently offer to clients? What do you think your clients would say if asked to describe your firm's value? What areas would be known versus unknown? You will have an opportunity to get more insight into these questions in Part II of the book, using the ClientWise Conversation™, but now is a great time to start considering your firm's value and the way your clients perceive it.

REFRAME #5: I BUILD A LEGACY BUSINESS THAT SERVES MULTIPLE GENERATIONS TO COME

For some advisors, it's natural to operate on the premise that your business will run as long as you do, and then, when you choose to walk away, it will be time to close the doors. The alternative—creating a succession plan, hiring the right advisors to follow in your footsteps, and taking the time to develop and mentor these advisors—is not necessarily attractive to the advisor who gets a thrill from winning business or running the numbers but not necessarily from mentoring the next generation. What's more, it's resource intensive to build your business to outlast you. Yet, the best in the business are finding a way to do just that.

The reasons are twofold. First, the best in the business recognize that to win the most clients, they need to have advisors who can work with all kinds of people, across every adult age group, rather than serving as the one and only advisor for each and every client. Today, an advisor's potential clients span four generations: the greatest generation, the boomers, the Gen Xers, and the millennials. Advisors who are the best in the business realize that younger clients have their own way of operating that may best be catered to by advisors of a younger generation, too. Some of these younger clients don't want to work with "Daddy's broker." The best in the business are making sure that these folks don't have to.

Second, the best in the business see the unique value of their experience and expertise and don't want to let them slip away when they choose to retire or step away from the business. There's no replacement for the body of knowledge that an advisor has developed over the decades as the industry has grown and changed: the ability to recognize trends and patterns, given that history repeats itself; the capacity to construct an investment portfolio rather than follow model portfolios; an understanding of the bond market; or the emotional intelligence of how to communicate with people.

The industry needs that wisdom to be passed on, as there is a scarcity of younger advisors joining the industry. According to Accenture, only 5 percent of U.S. financial advisors are younger than 30 years old.[5] In part, this is because there has been a trend, post-2008, for firms to hire experienced advisors from existing firms rather than recruiting and training younger individuals out of college. In addition, there is some speculation that grads are less interested in applying for these positions.[6]

Don't we owe it to our industry, to the public, and to ourselves to mentor the next generation of advisors and to pass our knowledge on to them, so they can continue to serve and support and we can enjoy the peace of mind that comes with passing on a legacy? Financial well-being enables the accomplishment of so much else: from being able to take care of one's family and send children to college to being able to invest in philanthropy. That's part of what makes advising a noble profession. If we hold our role to be invaluable in people's lives, then we need to treat our profession with the respect it deserves, helping it to live on in the next generation of well-prepared advisors. The best in the business—who are defined by more than just assets under management—understand this.

KEY CONCEPT

It may be most comfortable to work with peers as clients and not worry about what happens once you leave the advising business, but clients need and deserve to be more than your current paycheck. To truly elevate the wealth management profession, serve your clients, and leave a positive legacy, look to the future and mentor the next generation of advisors for your clients' sake as well as the future of wealth advising.

 Top 10 Secrets of the Best in the Business

While we're busy learning from the best in the business, let's go beyond the five reframes of the top advisors. Here is my top 10 list of what the best in the business are doing right now, including the five reframes but going further. I can tell you from coaching and training thousands of advisors since 2006 that the following practices are true of most of them.

The best in the business . . .

1. are intensely focused on growth and are willing to engage in a reframe.

2. understand that they cannot go it alone in today's world and that building a strong team is essential.

3. have already expanded their definition of wealth management to include a more comprehensive approach that has planning at its foundation.

4. are willing to take the time to get clear on how they uniquely define wealth management services offered by their firm.

5. are clear about their unique value proposition rather than just having a canned elevator speech.

6. have conditioned clients to understand the real value of their advisory firm, getting them invested in what the firm has to offer and turning them into loyal advocates.

7. know how important it is to attract human capital and are willing to invest in the process of finding the right individuals for the team.

(Continued)

(Continued)

8. have stopped selling to clients and are truly partnering.
9. believe in the importance of leadership development for themselves and their teams, moving folks on a trajectory from sales to technical expertise to leadership.
10. are comfortable partnering with other professionals to support clients across the full wealth management spectrum.

CONCLUSION

The best in the business know that continual improvement is essential to success. They are open to reframing themselves today and tomorrow, as needed, to meet the demands of their clients, the marketplace, and the industry. Remember only this, and you will be well on your way to operating at top capacity. Whether it's in the realm of how they manage client relationships, what kind of financial instruments and services they offer, or the way in which they develop their teams to be more robust and innovative, the top advisors place a value on growth and improvement that ensures they are attractive to existing and new clients alike. It reminds me of the story of the lion and gazelle.

As the story goes, every morning in Africa, a gazelle wakes up and it knows it has to run faster than the slowest lion or it will be eaten. Every day in Africa, a lion wakes up, and it knows it has to run faster than the slowest gazelle or it will starve. The point of the story is this: It doesn't matter if you are a lion or a gazelle—every day you've got to wake up and be running. How does this relate to the advisor? Regardless of your channel, the environment in which you operate is in constant flux—your clients, your profession, and your industry. So if you don't plan on changing, well . . . plan to be outrun.

I know, that sounds terrible, doesn't it? But there's truth to it. Our industry is constantly moving and evolving, with new regulations being added, the demographics of our clients changing (younger, female, ethnically diverse), and clients expecting more and new things from their advisors. To meet the consequent demands, advisors have got to get up and start moving.

Top advisors are in search of continual growth and have their ears to the ground on trends. They have open minds, can see possibility, and enjoy a capacity for creative thinking as well as change. All of these things allow top advisors and advisory firms to recognize the trends of today and respond to them. Lifelong learning, paired with insight into the trends of today, is what keeps the best the best.

You can create your own success by learning from others who lead the way, because there is truly a slice of the pie available to every advisor who is willing to adapt and reframe for tomorrow's world. With a realization of how expansive wealth management really is and an interest in connecting with clients' vast needs, there is fascinating, meaningful, and impactful work available for every interested financial advisor.

If you want to increase the number of clients that you serve, if you want to increase your revenue, if you want to increase profits, and if you want to build a business that truly has enterprise value and is really sustainable, then you have to change and improve. You have to really care about how you are being framed, and you have to be able to make a reframe when necessary. The Japanese call this process of continual improvement *kaizen*.[7] If you have a bigger future in mind, then you have to care about what people think about your brand. This is what the best in the business know and are acting on every single day.

The five reframes of the best in the business provide a roadmap for how you can best focus on growing and improving. The chapters that follow will take a deeper look at each of these reframes.

NOTES

1. David B. Armstrong, CFA, personal interview, March 6, 2015, transcript, p. 3.
2. Geri Eisenman Pell, personal interview, March 10, 2015, transcript, pp. 5–6.
3. Ibid., p. 8.
4. International Coaching Federation, "Core Competencies," accessed February 23, 2015, www.coachfederation.org/credential/landing.cfm?ItemNumber=2206&navItemNumber=576.
5. Accenture, *Advisor Succession Planning: Managing the Retirement of Baby Boomer Advisors,* 2013, accessed February 27, 2015, www.accenture.com/SiteCollectionDocuments/PDF/Accenture-CM-AWAMS-POV-Advisor-Succession-Planning-Final-Mar2013-web.pdf, p. 5.
6. Rachel Abrams, "A Hunt to Find the Next Generation of Financial Advisors." *DealBook* (blog), *New York Times*, June 24, 2014, http://dealbook.nytimes.com/2014/06/24/a-hunt-to-find-the-next-generation-of-financial-planners/?_r=0.
7. Kaizen Institute, "What is Kaizen?," accessed February 27, 2015, www.kaizen.com/about-us/definition-of-kaizen.html.

CHAPTER **3**

Death of a Salesman/ Saleswoman and Rise of the Wealth Advisor

One of the most significant problems financial advisors face is that the public does not know what they actually do. A person gets handed a business card from an advisor affiliated with a broker-dealer and assumes the advisor sells investments. A person receives a phone call from an advisor affiliated with an insurance agency and believes it precedes an insurance sale. But often, these frames and perceptions are outdated or inaccurate.

The current perceptual frame of the vast majority of the public is that most financial advisors are simply salespeople or that they only handle financial transactions. The thinking tends to be that the type of product, sale, or other financial transaction is limited to the business that the parent organization has historically done. The public doesn't realize that the wirehouse advisor might offer financial planning, providing a goals-based approach to designing a wealth strategy, or that the agent affiliated with an insurance company offers other services beyond insurance that include a financial planning approach. They don't distinguish between wealth management and investment management, or know that their current advisor can probably do far more for them than he or she is already doing. To be frank, when it comes to understanding what advisors do, the public is fairly uninformed.

The blame for this lack of understanding lies squarely with those of us in the financial services profession. Is it realistic to expect the public to have followed the evolution of our industry from a selling profession to an advising profession to a partnering profession? Is the public responsible for understanding the practical ramifications of new federal regulations and legislation on the way we do business, what we call ourselves, and how we are able to serve them? The answer to both questions is a clear no. In an industry as technical, complex, and ever-changing as financial services, it is up to advisors and financial services organizations to educate the public and clients on the function and value of wealth management advisors.

This reality gets at the heart of the challenge for advisors today: They are framed all the time by the very people they want to serve. More often than not, the client or potential client's frame is a misframe that leads to lost opportunity and lost business because clients are turned off by salespeople, they don't realize the full value they can attain by working with advisors, or both.

The best in the business have discovered that the sales frame is an important area to reframe. They've moved from the old frame of "I sell to my clients" to the new frame of "I partner with my clients." This chapter will explore that reframe in depth.

THE MIS-FRAME

Yes, it is true: Advisors have been framed as part of one of the least trusted groups in America—salespeople. It's not my intent to give financial advisors or salespeople a bad rap. However, all we have to do is think of the unlikable Willy Loman character in Arthur Miller's play *Death of a Salesman*, or the stereotype of the aggressive, self-serving used-car salesman to be reminded of the negative images that get associated with sales.

Because the public tends to think of the work of financial advisors as revolving around selling investments, life insurance, financial plans, and so on, every negative image associated with sales is, on a regular basis, automatically assigned to the advisor: pushy, self-interested, inauthentic, untrustworthy, obnoxious—you name it. As a result and without even opening one's mouth, the advisor who hangs a business shingle, affiliates with a brokerage firm, or hands out a business card has been framed.

What's more, when the financial services industry takes a misstep that shows up in the news headlines, the "greedy salesperson" frame is merely reinforced. Also reinforced is the idea that the industry (and therefore most financial advisors) is only interested in how much money can be made off of people.

In addition to the potential negative connotation of selling, the selling approach no longer accurately captures what advisors do. Today, wealth management advisors are doing financial planning, estate planning, tax minimization, and many other wealth-related activities, but the public often assumes that these individuals are simply selling investments because that is what many in the industry used to do. It's unfortunate because advisors lose an opportunity to provide more to their clients, and clients miss out on an opportunity to be served more comprehensively.

KEY CONCEPT

Most people do not realize that financial advisors no longer merely sell products; rather, advisors partner with clients to help them manage wealth and meet financial goals. It is up to financial advisors to clear up this misperception.

THE ROOTS OF THE INDUSTRY

The public has come by the negative salesperson frame honestly. In the early days of the profession (around the 1920s), the advisor was called "the customer's man" or the "customer's broker." The job of the customer's man was to place and take orders and to buy bonds and stocks. The customer's man sold investments to clients. Along the same lines, an insurance agent in this time period was called a "special agent." What a special agent did was sell life insurance products to customers.

Over time, the customer's man became "the stockbroker." The stockbroker also took orders from the client, managed the account, and bought and sold securities. As time went on, this financial professional became known as "the account executive." Whether the advisor was a customer's broker, a stockbroker, or an account executive, he or she was still an agent in the business of sales. The advisor in these times made money by buying and selling stocks, bonds, insurance, and other financial instruments to clients and by earning a commission or fee on the sale itself. The incentive was for the agent to buy and sell, all while making money for his or her client to retain the right to keep trading the client's account. The idea of financial planning as a whole or comprehensive wealth management had not yet come into play for the industry.

At the time, there was also a series of "county roads." If you got started in the business by joining an insurance firm, you sold life insurance. If you got started in a "boiler room" selling stocks and bonds, you were a broker. If you got started with the old IDS (Investors Diversified Services, Inc.), for example, you sold financial plans. Each of these individual firms primarily sold one product. Each product was its own individual county road.

The Glass-Steagall Act of 1933 changed things forever when it allowed a merger of professions, so that bankers could sell investment products, investment professionals could sell life insurance, and life insurance people could do financial planning. Suddenly, the service roads of the industry merged together onto a superhighway. Insurance agents began selling investment plans, investment managers began selling banking products, and bankers were all of a sudden selling investment products. Even the independent planners who might have been investment managers were helping clients minimize taxes by working with their clients' estate planners and writing insurance policies. The individual-product sale was over. The role of the wealth advisor was born.

KEY CONCEPT

The 1933 Glass-Steagall Act laid the groundwork for the profession of wealth advising by allowing bankers, life insurance agents, investment managers, and other professionals to sell multiple kinds of financial products.

After World War II, financial planning was born to meet the growing needs of Americans.[1] Suddenly, financial professionals were doing more than selling: They were helping clients create a financial roadmap for the future.

During the next few decades, the work of financial professionals continued to gain credibility as the industry organized to provide technical training and designations. Suddenly, multiple designations appeared in the industry. Members of the profession obtained CFPs, CHFCs, and CLUs; they earned CIMA Chartered Professional Wealth Advisor certifications. All of these designations helped to build some level of efficacy for an industry that was starving for a clearer identity and for credibility. The industry was also slowly but surely moving away from sales.

A further critical development occurred in 1969 when 13 individuals met in Chicago (predecessors to the Certified Financial Planner Board of Standards) and developed the notion that the public could gain value from a "profession that integrated knowledge and practices from the many, often-fragmented areas of the financial services industry."[2] The role of the advisor as a supportive expert who helped the client understand varying pieces of the financial industry—beyond investments—emerged. The move toward wealth management was underway, albeit without the name yet.

The trajectory of evolution faced by professionals in the industry is captured in Figure 3.1.

SALES, NO MORE

There was a time when the financial professional as salesperson was enough. In fact, as late as the 1980s, the stockbroker was a symbol of American success. The baby boomers working with them wanted the

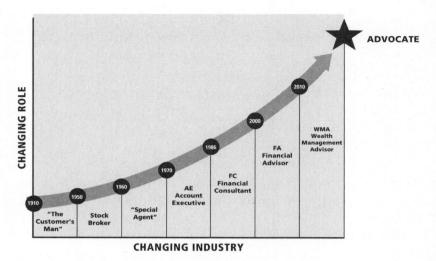

Figure 3.1 Evolving Role of the Financial Advisor

best of everything, including the best advice about which stocks to choose for their portfolios. Stockbrokers were held in high regard by the boomers, who were outearning their parents and transforming the economy in the process.

Then, during the 1990s, the boomers discovered the Internet, and many started doing their own trades online. What's more, after 30 years of brute-force traditional sales marketing from advisors, consisting of millions of cold calls a day, the public had become burned out on the sales approach that financial people had often provided to them. In addition, the public was smart enough to recognize that they could save the broker's commission by buying and selling on their own.

Suddenly, brokers-as-salespeople were needed less and less, and so these professionals transformed themselves into financial advisors, offering a more consultative and needs-based approach. However, many newly minted "advisors" were still essentially operating as salespeople, identifying their clients' needs to position products for sale. They were trying to do the same work disguised under a new name, even though the demands of the marketplace had changed. The sales approach was often endemic to the whole organization, a sign of the organizational strategy at large and an indicator of the culture of the industry.

Being a broker or a consultative seller is no longer enough. Today, the boomers are approaching retirement in large numbers and are leading increasingly complex lives. They need someone who can help them achieve not only their financial goals but also their life goals. They expect better service with lower fees. They've been through the ups and downs of the market and are skeptical of sales pitches. In response to the boomers' higher expectations, a new type of investment professional is being born.

The need for a new kind of advisor is not just due to boomers, though. Today's clientele—boomers, Gen Xers, and millennials alike—is sophisticated and different. In a flattening world where vertical hierarchies are transforming into horizontal relationships, the client expects to be brought into the planning process, not to be told to simply trust and accept the advisor's stock picks and financial recommendations. What's more, clients want to work with a financial professional who knows how to match goals with planning and investing.

In the old days, when investing was still out of reach and clouded in mystery for the mainstream person, clients needed their brokers and advisors to guide them on investments and to effect transactions for them. I can still remember giving a seminar in the late 1990s in Wichita, Kansas, regarding a privatization fund my firm was selling. Heavy snow was falling as I pulled into the parking lot and I remember thinking that no one would show up in such bad weather. Instead, 250 people made up my audience, and I developed laryngitis because I had to talk loudly enough for everyone to hear me. Similar bad weather at a seminar in Oklahoma City did not deter folks from attending that time, either. Neither did other such circumstances all over the country. People were coming to these seminars because they had to come; it was the only way to get information at the time.

Today, people don't have to come to these presentations or seek out advisors to get information on investing: They can get it on the Internet. There they can research, buy, and sell investments, managing their own portfolios with ease.

For the youngest generations, who are tech-savvy digital natives, online money management comes naturally. When one of my sons was in high school, for example, he surprised me one day by letting me know he had started managing his own investment portfolio online. While we had had some conversations along the way to set the stage for his interest in finances, the initiative was all his own and he had no trouble getting set up online. The world is different now. The reality is that 20, 30, 40, and 50 years ago, financial advisors were needed to effect transactions, make trades, and sell stuff; today, those services are no longer necessary.

KEY CONCEPT

Today's clients are sophisticated consumers with experience in managing their money and investments online. An experienced advisor can offer this new breed of client help in planning out what steps he or she needs to take to meet his or her financial goals.

WELCOME TO THE WORLD OF WEALTH ADVISING

With the "death of the salesman" in financial services, we are seeing the "birth of the wealth advisor." Christopher P. Jordan, founder and CEO of LEXCO Wealth Management, has seen this transformation take place in his own career.

Prior to founding LEXCO, Jordan worked as a partner in an advisory firm that placed a heavy emphasis on sales quotas and selling loaded mutual funds and other commission-based products. Interested in taking a more holistic approach to wealth management, he started his own firm that focused on service rather than sales. "With high-net-worth clients, you've got to offer something more than just a product," says Jordan. By taking a comprehensive approach to meeting his clients' needs, Jordan has created a highly successful practice. LEXCO Wealth Management has been ranked the number seven branch in the nation with National Planning Corporation,[3] and Jordan's now 17-person firm has been ranked "three years running as one of the top 10 offices in the nation at his Broker/Dealer."[4]

For Jordan, being a wealth advisor means bringing together a team of people to help his clients achieve their goals. He communicates regularly with a broad network of estate planners, insurance specialists, CPAs, attorneys, mortgage experts, and other professionals who can help his clients create an integrated financial plan. "In today's marketplace, you've got be different," says Jordan. "Our team-based approach is one way in which we differentiate our firm while helping our clients simplify their financial lives."[5]

Because Jordan makes it easier for his clients to reach their goals, his clients see him as a trusted advisor rather than simply a salesman. He has shifted from the old frame of "I provide my clients with one particular financial service" to "I provide my clients with comprehensive wealth management that begins with outcomes-based financial planning."

KEY CONCEPT

Finding a way to differentiate yourself and/or your firm from others in the field is a key to success.

Having started LEXCO in 1999, Jordan has been an early leader in the movement to evolve the financial services industry away from sales and into holistic wealth management. Unlike some professionals in the industry who have caught on to the title change from financial advisor to wealth management advisor without actually deepening their practices, Jordan has built a firm that can deliver on its promise to help clients manage the full breadth of their wealth.

COACHING CORNER

Take a moment to reflect on the philosophy and approach behind how you serve your clients. Where are you possibly still stuck in a sales approach? Where are you succeeding at providing comprehensive wealth management?

▼ How Should Advisors Charge Today?

It's a dirty little secret, but I believe that what is really holding us back as an industry is the way that many financial advisors are compensated. Many

(Continued)

(Continued)

financial advisors receive the largest percentage of their compensation on the basis of managing a client's portfolio. Right there, advisors are incentivized to focus on investments rather than goal setting, planning, or any of the other diverse areas of a client's wealth picture.

The industry can rise up to meet this new opportunity to manage wealth when it becomes clearer about charging clients a fee not just on the assets that are being managed but rather on the time and delivery of the wealth plan and strategy. Inclusive in that wealth plan and strategy is the design, implementation, and delivery of all things related to wealth management. Advisors need to be able to charge a higher fee when they provide more services.

As we evolve from a transactional industry where we sold lots of products to an industry where we are advising rather than selling, we need to move beyond the old compensation structure of charging a fee for the assets under management to what some advisors are already doing—charging clients fees for helping them with all things related to their wealth.

A New Way to Benchmark

At the core of wealth management is a financial plan that is paired with the client's goals and vision for the future. When I worked at Alliance Bernstein, we called it "benchmarking the beach house." If the client's goal was to buy a vacation home, we created a financial plan that took into consideration the amount of money that would be needed to eventually make the purchase, and we designed a plan that included the monthly savings and time frame required to reach this goal. If a client was saving for a child's college education and tuition was expected to cost a quarter million dollars, we would determine how much money the client needed to save each month to get there x number of years from now.

Another way to think of this is benchmarking to a family index or a personal index—to those goals that are important to the client and the client's family. Instead of just putting a lot of money in a portfolio and looking to get the most performance out of it (benchmarking to the S&P or other index), the wealth advisor helps the client create a plan that supports specific client goals—a plan that pegs to the family index, the personal index, or that list of things that represent the client's vision of success. In a big-picture sense, a wealth advisor provides guidance around the design of the client's future and how personal wealth will help the client achieve what it is he or she wants to achieve. The wealth advisor serves as a guide, certainly possessing all of the technical competencies needed to support the client but also having the relational ability to help the client through the process of discovering how he or she wants the future to look and how the advisor can actively participate in managing wealth to get there.

This is where the coaching aspect of wealth management comes in. I'm not referring to coaching in the athletic sense, where the coach tells the player on the field which plays to run and which goals to achieve, but the kind of coaching we see in business, where executive coaches partner with leaders to help them set their own agenda and then achieve it through planning, support, and accountability. Today's wealth advisor allows the client to take more of a leadership role in the partnership than has ever occurred in the past. Together, they are coauthors and cocreators in the design of a wealth strategy that supports the client's goals and vision for the future. The client brings the dreams, personal insight, and motivation to engage; the advisor brings the technical expertise, professional insight, and relational capacity to guide the client through the discovery and execution of the plan.

KEY CONCEPT

Today's wealth advisors function as coaches, helping clients achieve their dreams and goals by offering professional expertise, insight, and support.

THE eXchange™

Online Tool 3.1: Ten Reasons Your Clients Will Love You for Offering True Wealth Management

Visit the eXchange™ to discover 10 reasons your clients will love you for offering true wealth management. Feel free to adapt this list to your brand and to include it in

(Continued)

(*Continued*)

your firm's marketing literature so you can share it with clients and teach them more about why comprehensive wealth management sets you apart from other firms.

 INDUSTRY INSIGHT: USING THE FINANCIAL PLAN TO GAUGE SUCCESS

David B. Armstrong, CFA, president and cofounder of Monument Wealth Management, can still remember the day a disgruntled potential client called him and asked if he could come in for an appointment with Monument because he wasn't happy with his current financial advisor.[6] When Armstrong inquired about why the man on the line—let's call him Mike—was unhappy with his advisor, his answer was simple: "I don't think they are making me enough money."

Armstrong replied by asking, "What kind of return do you need in order to feel like you are making a lot of money?" and Mike explained that actually, he didn't know, it was just how he felt about the situation. Mike took another moment to think and then clarified things further. He explained how the S&P 500 had been up 30 percent the previous year, while Mike's portfolio had only gone up by 14 percent. He did not feel good about that and blamed his advisors.

Armstrong did not disagree, and here's why. As it turns out, Mike's firm had not worked with him to create a financial plan. Armstrong shared that if Mike had had a plan, he would know exactly how to gauge whether his firm was helping him achieve success. So Armstrong asked Mike, "What if your plan only called for your portfolio to be up 7 percent and you were up 14 percent? Would you feel good about that?" Within that context, the client's answer was yes.

The moral of this story, according to Armstrong, is to begin with a financial plan and then use that plan—rather than the S&P 500—to benchmark success. The financial plan is so valuable because it serves as a reminder to people on a quarterly basis what their long-term goal is and how they're going to get there. It allows the advisor and client to assess whether true success is being achieved and signals when the wealth management strategy needs to be adjusted.

As the financial services industry moves away from being sales based, there is a huge opportunity for wealth advisors to start having what I call *larger conversations* with clients. Larger conversations include discussing things like

- How would you like your life to look in five years? Ten years? Twenty years?
- What wealth strategy and financial plan can we create together to help you get there?
- What are all of the pieces of the wealth picture that we need to consider to make sure we maximize success?
- What parts of the plan are you most comfortable with? Are you willing to commit to and engage with the plan? Is the plan realistic? If not, how do we need to adjust the plan?

Advisors are used to the idea of financial planning. It's the discovery piece related to helping the client verbalize the vision behind the plan that's the newer piece for most advisors. This is where advisors can bring new value to clients—by using coaching and relational skills to elicit what the Kinder Institute refers to as "the human side of financial planning."[7]

The Kinder Institute refers to the process as *life planning*:

In Life Planning we discover a client's deepest and most profound goals through a [. . .] process of structured and non-judgmental inquiry. Then, using a mix of professional and advanced relationship skills, we inspire clients to pursue their aspirations, discuss and resolve obstacles, create a concrete financial plan, and provide ongoing guidance as clients accomplish their objectives.[8]

In the past, advisors were technical experts helping clients buy, sell, and trade to make more money; today, advisors are more than technical experts, and their goal is more than sales. Advisors are partnering with their clients to increase their wealth in ways that match their unique goals. Coaching skills are a powerful way to unlock a client's goals, motivation, engagement, and commitment.

New approaches to advising bring new challenges, but the good news is that advisors don't have to start from scratch in developing the discovery process. Instead, they can borrow tricks and tools of the trade right from the executive coaching profession, which for years has been helping leaders identify goals, create action plans, and achieve them through support and accountability. It's the same coaching process that ClientWise explores with our financial professional clients every day; this book will provide these coaching techniques to help advisors engage in a successful discovery process with clients.

The time has come for advisors to start having much larger, more impactful conversations with clients, and to consistently do so. No longer is advising just about managing people's money or selling them a financial plan or convincing them to buy a life insurance policy. It's all about *partnering* with clients to help them identify their unique goals for the future, collaborating to create a goal-based financial plan that the client is able to commit to, and checking in over time to ensure the plan is on track and working.

COACHING CORNER

What does it mean to you to truly partner with your clients? Think of or write down five ways in which you enjoy partnering with clients and/or you would like to partner with clients in the future.

Three Reasons to Make the Shift from Sales or Consultant to Wealth Advisor

From the customer's man, stockbroker, and account executive to the financial consultant, financial advisor, and now wealth advisor, those in the financial services profession have a huge opportunity to make a fundamental difference in people's lives while growing their practices in the process. Here are three reasons to make the shift.

1. By partnering with clients rather than selling to them or even directing them, advisors unlock the collaborative power of a team. By pairing the advisor's expertise with the client's interests and motivations, the chances of maximizing wealth grow exponentially.

2. By engaging clients in a discovery process focused on setting goals, the advisor ensures that the financial plan gets constructed

in a way that matches the unique needs of the client. Again, this increases client motivation to participate; just as important, it ensures client satisfaction when the right goals are ultimately reached.

3. By shifting to an approach of comprehensive wealth management rather than remaining focused on just one piece of the client's financial picture, advisors create huge value for the client who operates in a busy world and hardly has the time or expertise to manage on his or her own the many elements of his or her wealth.

As a bonus, because the client has co-created the plan with the advisor, advisors don't have to spend time getting the client to commit to the plan, as the client is already on board.

CONCLUSION

It is time for the death of the salesman and the rise of the wealth advisor. It is time for advisors to move away from a transactional sales approach, and even the consulting approach, and toward forming deeper relationships with clients. It is time for advisors to serve clients by stepping into the lead role of coordinating the many professionals that are needed to deliver true wealth management. It is time, too, to change the way advisors charge for their services while redefining the value they provide. And it is time to develop an intimate understanding of each client's unique needs as clients move toward a future just their own. While sales will always remain a part of our job as advisors, being wealth advisors means spending less time selling products and more time marketing ourselves as trusted advisors and then delivering on that promise.

Although many advisors have moved along a trajectory from sales to financial advising and now to overall wealth management, many clients are still stuck framing advisors as salespeople. That mind-set affects clients' willingness to engage with the advisor; it affects their ability to seek the services advisors provide. Finally, it limits clients' ability to tell others about the advisor's value. It is up to advisors to educate clients, their other trusted advisors, and the public on the vast new ways that they can support clients. The reward will be more business, more introductions from the other professionals, and, ultimately, more loyal client advocates who are willing to help their advisors find additional clients. The reward will be an industry that is elevated as the public begins to understand the significant service that advisors provide to the community at large.

The lesson for advisors may be just as much about learning to see and frame themselves differently—not as transactional agents, but as partners with the client and as custodians of the client's whole wealth picture. For some, this very well might reveal the opportunity to add that more human element to the picture through stronger relational work; for others, it might be the opportunity to provide more technical expertise for clients. The end result will be more satisfied clients and more satisfied advisors, too, who are engaged in meaningful work that yields results and has an impact.

As advisors and as an industry, it is time to rise up and give more to our clients. We need to shift from selling to supporting, from telling to discovery, from hierarchy to partnership, and from one piece of the wealth pie to the whole wealth picture. Today, the value proposition for the client is in that partnership. Those advisors who are able to evoke from the client insights and desires about what they want their wealth to do for them will have the competitive advantage.

In this new phase of the profession, managing money, selling life insurance policies, writing financial plans, rebalancing portfolios, minimizing taxes, and providing banking services all become the technical back-end piece of advising. The front-end piece—the piece that is most powerful—is forward-facing partnering and communicating with the client.

The truth is that being a salesperson is not noble. But helping individuals discover, pursue, and achieve their goals is. As clients achieve their goals, they have the ability to pay it forward, and everyone benefits.

NOTES

1. "About CFP Board." CFP Board website (n.d.), CFP Board's Early Days section, accessed May 29, 2015, www.cfp.net/about-cfp-board/about-cfp-board/history.

2. Ibid.

3. Financial Advisor Profile: Christopher Paul Jordan, President & CEO." LEXCO Wealth Management website (n.d.), accessed May 29, 2015, http://lexcowealth. com/advisors/christopher-p-jordan.

4. Ibid.

5. This information is being cited from an article written by Ray Sclafani that is titled "From Broker to Facilitator," which can be found at: www.clientwise.com/ leadership/articles/evolution-of-the-facilitator.

6. David B. Armstrong, CFA, personal interview, March 6, 2015, transcript, pp. 5, 12.

7. The Kinder Institute of Life Planning website (n.d.), "What Is Life Planning?" section, accessed May 29, 2015, www.kinderinstitute.com/professional.html.

8. Ibid.

CHAPTER **4**

The Big, Fat Lie

Some frames, like the advisor-as-salesperson frame, are problematic because they limit clients' ideas about what the advisor can do for them, reducing profits in the process. Other frames may be right on track—well placed and with good intentions—yet if the advisor fails to live up to them, client trust gets broken, damaging the advisor's reputation. We'll look at one such frame—that of "we'll always be there for you"—in this chapter.

It's a strange irony: Advisors regularly frame themselves as planners for their clients, but paradoxically, many advisors fail to plan—not for their clients but for themselves and their businesses when it comes to continuity, succession, and longevity. As asset management and distribution analytics firm Cerulli Associates has indicated, only 29 percent of advisors have a succession plan at all.[1] A full 59 percent of advisors within five years of retirement do not have a succession plan.[2] Those advisors who do have a succession plan may just be fooling themselves into thinking it's adequate. The plan may look good on paper, but when put to the reality test, it can easily fall apart, as will become clear later in this chapter.

KEY CONCEPT

The best advisors have plans in place not only for their clients but also for themselves and their businesses, ensuring that if the advisor ever has to step away from work, the clients will smoothly transition to their new advisor or team.

WE'LL ALWAYS BE THERE FOR YOU . . . UNTIL WE AREN'T

Picture the following television commercial to gain insight into the "we'll always be there for you" frame. The screen shows a young married couple bringing their first child home from the hospital. It flashes to the baby's fifth birthday party, with the happy mom and dad giving their child a new bike. Next thing on the screen is the child's college graduation, followed by footage of the adult child having her own child, with the loving grandparents nearby. The commercial closes with all three generations sitting on a bench outside an assisted living facility. The tagline of a financial services company appears at the bottom of the screen as a voiceover promises, "We'll be there."

This commercial, representative of those we've seen from financial services companies over the years, conveys the promise that every advisor makes to his or her clients, whether overtly or implicitly: the promise to be there for the client through all of life's transitions, at each and every turn where financial support is needed. Whether it's through TV, print, or online advertising; marketing materials; or the conversations advisors have with clients, most advisors and financial services firms court and reassure clients on the basis of this premise that they can be relied on no matter how much time passes or how uncertain life becomes. The reality is, however, that many advisors do not have an effective plan to ensure that the client will truly be taken care of over the years. I call this failure *the big, fat lie*.

Clients would be shocked to know that their financial advisor might not actually have a plan in place if he or she were to become ill or disabled or pass away, leaving both the clients and the advisor's family unattended. A client who has signed on with an advisor who's middle aged may be horrified 15 years down the road when that advisor dies during the client's retirement years with no satisfactory replacement in place. Clients who have been told for years by their advisor that another firm is ready to take over in the case of illness or absence may be disappointed to learn when this contingency comes true that they don't like working with the replacement or that the replacement has changed plans and does not want to work with them.

I'm reminded of a busy, successful advisor who lost sight in one eye and then the other. Although he had a partner, his partner decided that he no longer wanted to work with the advisor, and the advisor could not serve his clients on his own with his new disability. His clients were suddenly without an advisor, left to fend for themselves. The noble promise of the advisor is to be there for the client through all of life's transitions—loyal and steadfast, like a rock-solid partner, rather than an opportunist who is merely renting the relationship. It's the way that advisors frame themselves for clients, directly or indirectly. Unfortunately, even the most well-meaning advisors sometimes fail to fulfill this pledge and thus fall prey to telling a big, fat lie that they will always be there for clients, when at some point, in reality, they simply can't or won't.

KEY CONCEPT

If you are framing yourself as an advisor who can help clients prepare for a lifetime of financial challenges, it is incumbent upon you to prepare for a time when you cannot or will not be working with your clients directly anymore. If you do not make adequate succession plans, you are lying to your clients.

Sunbathing in Florida at the Clients' Expense

The example of Mick will give more clarity on how advisors are challenged to follow through on their promises to clients and how they sometimes render that promise a big, fat lie. Mick is a financial advisor who runs his own firm. He has been in the industry for 35 years and has had his own business for 25. Mick has a group of more than 100 clients whom he has served for many years. He has more than

$150 million in assets under management and a sales assistant that knows the clients, perhaps better than Mick does. Mick has long enjoyed running his own operation because it allows him to work personally with his clients, as he feels will best benefit them, without being beholden to a larger corporate strategy that may or may not jive with his clients' needs and lives.

Because Mick has always put his clients' needs first, even going beyond his commitment to them by making house calls and working during holidays, they absolutely love him. He is authentic, reliable, and personable. Mick's clients feel they can trust him now and into the future. He has always told them that he will be with them through all of life's stages, and he certainly has been there to provide support as his clients have bought homes, put their children through college, and dealt with the illnesses of spouses and aging parents.

But at age 62, as Mick is starting to wind down professionally, the question is, What will happen to his clients in the process? Mick has told his clients he will be there for them through all of life's big moments, but Mick is starting to disengage. The cold, hard facts are that Mick really wants to spend more time in Boca Raton and enjoy the sun while continuing to get paid as if he were working full time. How honest does he need to be with himself and his clients about his ability to serve them? Should Mick just keep taking his percentage while spending less and less time at the office, or should he make some changes to ensure that his clients are receiving all that they deserve, now and after Mick's gone?

It's a question that every advisor will eventually have to ask him- or herself as well, to ensure the best possible client outcomes and, frankly, to avoid engaging in any malfeasance. It's time for advisors to invest in the human capital needed to truly deliver for the client, or to be honest with clients about the degree to which they can serve.

How Good Is Your Succession Plan?

With the average age of financial advisors in America being 50.9 years old, Mick has lots of company.[3] Advisors across the land are graying, looking toward retirement, scaling back on clients, and figuring out how to transition out of their firms. The latest data from

Cerulli Associates reveals that 5 percent of wirehouse advisors are expected to retire in the next five years and 35 percent will retire in the next 10 years, while 25 percent of independent broker-dealers and 30 percent of registered investment advisors indicate that they will leave their practices or retire in the next 10 years. Across all channels, one in four advisors is expected to leave the industry in the next 10 years. Financial services clients across the land are going to be affected as their advisors disengage or drop out of the industry.

For advisors who do have a succession plan in place, the effectiveness of that plan can easily be called into question. Let's take a look at Mick's situation to understand how. Traditionally, advisors like Mick who run a small operation have put plans into place to transition out of their firms by creating a buy/sell agreement with another advisor who will take over in case of sickness, retirement, or death. While this is certainly a good alternative to having no agreement, noble advisors have got to ask themselves whether such an agreement is really enough.

COACHING CORNER

What does your succession plan look like today? How would you rate it on a scale of 1 to 5 (5 being best)? Be honest. Then pick three things you'd like to do to improve your succession plan in the coming year and mark time on your calendar to start making them happen.

THE eXchange™

Online Tool 4.1: Succession Planning Checklist

Visit the eXchange™ to download a Succession Planning Checklist for use or adaptation by your firm.

Take a moment to imagine how this all might play out not nearly as well as desired. Five years from now, Mick decides he is ready to retire. He triggers his buy/sell agreement with a younger advisor, Joe, and sends a letter to all of his clients, along with making a personal phone call to each, letting them know about his retirement and providing Joe's contact information to ensure continuity of support. This sounds fair, and it certainly meets a minimum standard of ethics. Yet how are Mick's clients going to feel when they learn that after years of working with Mick, they are now expected to switch to a completely different advisor at a different firm whose style is different than Mick's—right in the middle of their own important life changes? Are they going to feel a sense of comfort and connection with Joe, or are they going to feel like they've been dropped in the lap of a random new advisor that they may—or may not—like?

Further complicating the issue, Joe may discover that right now, he only has room to take on 10 new clients rather than Mick's 100. Or he may only want to work with those of Mick's clients who need financial planning and investment strategies support but not retirement advice or estate planning, as Mick was apt to provide. It's not unrealistic to think that Joe's firm has evolved since he and Mick first created their agreement or that Joe simply did not accurately predict what kind of new clients he'd like to take on when the time came, yet this will leave many of Mick's clients out in the cold. Mick—a dedicated, reliable, and caring advisor—is no longer able to deliver on the promise that his firm will be there for his clients through all of their life stages. As Mick's succession plan disintegrates under pressure, it becomes clear that well-intentioned Mick has peddled his clients a big, fat lie without ever meaning to.

KEY CONCEPT

Once you have a succession plan in place, revisit it regularly to make sure your arrangements are still realistic, and make any necessary adjustments.

I don't know a single advisor who would tell me that he or she is not focused on helping clients achieve their goals in the event of his or her absence. I've said it before and I'll say it again: The majority of advisors are principled, dedicated, and client-focused professionals.

They want the absolute best for their clients! Yet many of them are telling their clients a big, fat lie—that they will always be there for them, when in fact they have no succession plan or the one they do have in place isn't particularly strong. To operate with integrity and to fulfill the promise of the "we'll always be there for you" frame that most advisors convey to clients, advisors will need to take a look at their succession planning to assess how effective it really is. Ultimately, they will need to make a shift from the old frame of "I allow clients to rent my services until I choose to stop practicing" to "I build a legacy business that serves multiple generations to come."

 Will You Rust or Will You Rise?

Admittedly, there's a counterperspective to the headlines and statistics that proclaim that financial advisors are about to retire in droves. After traveling around the country and working with thousands of advisors, I have started to modify this theory to state that financial advisors are about to *semiretire* in droves. Instead of retiring, aging advisors are tending to hold on to the "good life" by maintaining their client roster and retaining the associated income stream while spending fewer hours engaged on the job. Voila! Semiretirement, here come the advisors. Who wants to stop working when you can make 1 percent on assets under management while spending mornings on the back nine and afternoons poolside? Sounds enticing.

A Loss of Legacy. Think of it this way. Not only are advisors doing a disservice to their clients if they disengage—clients get less of the advisor's time and attention and really will be lost when the advisor stops working completely—but they are also allowing their own businesses to decay instead of leaving behind a legacy. Is this the vision that most advisors have for their businesses—that the business will thrive while they are in the heart of their working years and then, as they age, the business will simply rust away? Some advisors will say they have support staff who will be there to fulfill the promises. However, in most instances, the support staff has not been developed to a point of being able to keep offering the same degree of service. What's more, the client often does not have a relationship with the staff,

(Continued)

(Continued)

is uninterested in being served by them, and will just choose to go elsewhere. This is the hard truth.

A Loss of Wisdom. One of my biggest fears, as a financial services veteran who cares about the industry, is that aging advisors will disengage more and more from their work without letting clients know that they've gone on indefinite hiatus and that there's no good backup waiting in the wings. For clients, it's the worst of all worlds, as their advisors become less hands-on in their approach without providing the client suitable supplementation to what they now can offer from the place of semiretirement. For the industry, mass semiretirement of advisors until they simply rust away would be a tragedy, too. Why? As older advisors drop out of the industry, their expertise and wisdom will be lost rather than passed on to the next generation. What a shame it would be—and a disservice to the industry and clients—to let so much technical, service, and relational savvy disappear.

The answer for aging and semiretiring advisors is to build out a team. Sounds like hard work at first, but once the team is in place, the seasoned advisor gains the freedom to work less and enjoy life more, while running a firm that can be bought down the road, internally or externally. That makes for a much better ending to the story for mature advisors than simply rusting away.

Rent-an-Advisor

It's not that advisors want to leave clients so they are hung out to dry. This approach of serving the client until the advisor can't serve the client anymore has often just been the way of things.

Right now, most advisors are set up so that they allow clients to rent the relationship with them. The client pays the advisor for his or her services until the advisor no longer can or will provide them, then the client is required to rent a new advisor.

However, there is an alternative to this approach—and the best in the business are already using it. It's about building a *team of professionals* to support the client and creating a firm culture that transcends the single advisor. Suddenly, the client is no longer renting one advisor but has access to an entire team for the long term, a team that won't expire when a single "lease" is up.

The advisors on that team have common values and work within a common culture, so if the need to switch advisors arises, the transition is far smoother than in the case of Mick's clients being sent cold turkey to Joe. Throughout the years, the client knows that there will be support regardless of whether his or her lead advisor has to step away due to illness or other circumstances.

Your clients depend on you for guidance now and into the future. They also hope that the money they've worked so hard to save will be managed well when their children inherit it, and they would love to see their kids go on to work with Mom and Dad's trusted advisor. What are you doing to make that happen?

KEY CONCEPT

One succession strategy is to have a team of professionals in place for the duration of the advisor–client relationship. This way, when the lead advisor steps out, the rest of the team is positioned to carry out the original promise of a lifetime of service.

COACHING CORNER

Imagine that you were forced to step away from your advising work for a long period. How would your clients be taken care of? What kind of plan do you have in place? What areas of your plan are strong? What areas of the plan could you stand to improve?

INDUSTRY INSIGHT: A PROMISE TO OFFER TRUE WEALTH MANAGEMENT

Another version of the big, fat lie is the promise by advisors to offer clients wealth management services when, in fact, they are delivering only partial wealth

(Continued)

(Continued)

management that focuses on one area of wealth alone, such as investments. In the past five years, the use of the term *wealth management* to describe the work that advisors do has become more and more commonplace. Yet it is often a case of rebranding without reframing, as firms have caught on to the desired industry lingo without making actual changes in the way they do business. For Rob Nelson, president of NorthRock Partners, the reframe for his work from more traditional financial advising to comprehensive wealth management was authentic.

For years, Nelson worked as a financial advisor for one of the largest financial services companies in the United States, where he learned the ins and outs of the business and grew from being a newbie advisor to a seasoned one. Nelson enjoyed the work and respected his firm but, over time, realized it was time for him to reframe himself so he could deliver on the inherent promise he felt he made to his clients to truly take care of them. He wanted to offer more comprehensive support than he could at his traditional advisory firm: tax planning and preparation, banking, bill payment, legal issues, and estate planning.

Nelson wanted to be able to support his clients in all aspects of their financial lives and with less confinement, so he took the leap and became a registered investment advisor. The good news was that Nelson now had the freedom to partner with any custodian in the financial services industry who he felt was right for his clients; the bad news was that he could work with any custodian in the financial services industry, which would be no small feat: Nelson and his new firm would now have to do everything on their own. The new challenges were worth it, however. "It ended up being one of the best decisions I've ever made," said Nelson.[4]

To successfully make the transition, Nelson spoke openly with his existing clients of 10 and 20 years and shared with them the direction his new firm would be going in and why. In becoming a registered investment advisor, Nelson explained, he would be gaining more flexibility to serve clients based on what they truly needed, not what Nelson's former organization happened to offer. The client response to Nelson's transition was overwhelmingly supportive. As it turned out, they never felt that they had a relationship with Nelson's former employer; rather, they felt that they had a relationship with him. His employer held their assets, but Nelson was their trusted advisor, and they felt confident that he could continue to be after he moved on to being an RIA. As Nelson explains, "It was actually a little less of an event for my clients than it was for me. They still needed to have a faith moment when it came down to moving their assets to another custodian and starting to work with us in a different way, but it went really well."[5]

Separating from his former firm made it easier for Nelson to frame himself accurately online. When clients shared his name with others, they would often Google him as a first point of contact. In the past, his former employer's website would naturally pop up, which had branding that was different from that of Nelson's personal style of advising. After the switch to being his own firm, a Google search would bring up NorthRock Partners, which immediately reflected Nelson's style of advising and offering true wealth management. He was able to create the desired client experience from the start.

With his new firm launched, Nelson was able to offer his clients a deeper relationship in banking, give true advice, gain clearer control of assets, help them with their legal and estate planning in a deeper way, and even do some of that trust work on site. His intention to deliver true wealth management had become a reality and was more than lip service. He knew it was a success by the way clients invited him into their lives. Nelson finds that when he's working with a professional athlete who's thinking about changing teams, the athlete wants his family there so they can participate in the discussion about what such a change would mean. If one of Nelson's corporate executive clients is considering changing to a new employer, he or she invites Nelson's team to be there. If a client has a divorce on the horizon, a lot of times it's the spouse and Nelson's team who know about it. It's the ultimate sign of trust, resulting from the "deep-rooted relationships"[6] that Nelson has developed with his clients. Nelson has been there for many challenging as well as feel-good moments during which his clients would say he has made a real difference in their lives. Goodbye, big, fat lie.

THE NEXT GENERATION OF ADVISORS

As noted earlier, there is currently a scarcity of young financial advisors in the industry, with only 5 percent of the 315,000 advisors working in the United States younger than 30.[7] This scarcity is believed to exist for a number of reasons. After the economic crisis of 2008–2009, many big firms stopped recruiting new grads and started hiring experienced advisors from other firms.[8]

Further, young people themselves appear to have little interest in joining the world of traditional financial advising. As Scott Smith, a Cerulli Associates director, puts it, "You're asking a 26-year-old to take his parents' phone book and convince all their friends to hand over substantial sums of money. Young people have a greater interest in being more holistic planners, and less transactional."[9] Enter opportunity, however. As the industry shifts more toward comprehensive wealth advising and away from a transactions-based approach, it may be a lure for the younger generation.

Younger advisors are certainly needed. As boomers get more and more ready to transfer their wealth to their Gen X and millennial children and as the millennials grow up into bona fide adults, the need for the next generation of advisors increases. The cold, hard truth is that most young people don't want to work with Daddy's broker. They need someone who understands the way they think, play, communicate, live, and work. What an opportunity this presents to savvy financial services firms who are willing to build a team of advisors that spans the generations. Doing so increases opportunities for business today as well as the opportunity to sell the firm down the line to an internal player.

Paul Pagnato, founder and managing director of Pagnato Karp, explains it like this: "Individuals like to work with and hire an advisor that they're similar to in age. There are a lot of studies done, and someone who is 28 or 30 years old typically wants to work with someone that's 30 years old. They don't want to work with someone who is 60 years old. I believe that is an issue and that's going to be a challenge in the marketplace."[10]

Pagnato believes this situation brings opportunity, too. With their ease in using and embracing technology, he sees Gen X and millennial advisors with plenty to offer clients as technology plays a greater role in how money is managed. He is optimistic, too, that "as the financial system is healed [post-2008], you'll see more advisors coming into the marketplace that are younger" as hiring trends increase.[11]

When asked what advice he would give to advisors in their 20s and 30s, Pagnato suggests that these young advisors train and enter the business as a fiduciary rather than associating with a broker-dealer. "I believe that is where the puck is going, that is clearly where all the regulators are going, [and] it is clearly where the assets are going," notes Pagnato. "You can look at all the data, and the money is flowing to the independents that are more embracive of the fiduciary standards [while] . . . society as a whole is becoming much more socially responsible . . . People want to work with companies that are doing the right thing, and that's what the fiduciary standard is all about. It's about doing the right thing."[12]

KEY CONCEPT

A tremendous opportunity exists for younger advisors: Not only do younger clients want to work with advisors who understand them, but having younger advisors on a financial services team helps put to rest older clients' and employers' succession fears.

CONCLUSION

For years, advisors have been framing themselves as able to serve clients through all of life's transitions and stages. Yet sadly, many of them are sole practitioners, and their businesses, which they worked so hard to build, will dry up and eventually fade away. This will leave clients scrambling in search of a new advisor to "rent" from a place of weakness and surprise rather than strength. These advisors are principled practitioners who value integrity, but they end up failing to fulfill their promise to always be there for clients.

The solution, as it turns out, is quite simple: Build a team of advisors that allows the advisor to create a robust business that survives—and thrives—even when the lead advisor steps away.

Once again, it's a call for all of us in the industry to be noble. If we really want to think about the financial services profession in a bigger way and if we are truly grateful for the great profession that we've had the pleasure to be part of, then it's incumbent upon us to really think about the successful service of the client. That means thinking about transitioning our roles now, with all the wisdom we've accumulated over the years, to other advisors on the team.

As advisors build a team and their clients grow comfortable with wanting to work with the team, advisors can work less, let the team do more, and increase the enterprise value of their business. That's something to celebrate!

NOTES

1. Accenture, *Advisor Succession Planning: Managing the Retirement of Baby Boomer Advisors,* 2013, accessed March 17, 2015, www.accenture.com/SiteCollectionDocuments/PDF/Accenture-CM-AWAMS-POV-Advisor-Succession-Planning-Final-Mar2013-web.pdf, p. 4, paras. 1–2.

2. Matthew Heimer, "Will Your Advisor Retire Before You Do?," *MarketWatch Encore* (blog), July 19, 2013, http://blogs.marketwatch.com/encore/2013/07/19/will-your-adviser-retire-before-you-do/.

3. *FA* Staff, "43% of Advisors Nearing Retirement, Says Cerulli," *Financial Advisor Online,* January 17, 2014, www.fa-mag.com/news/43--of-all-advisors-are-approaching-retirement--says-cerulli-16661.html.

4. Rob Nelson, personal interview, April 28, 2015, transcript, p. 2.

5. Rob Nelson, personal interview, April 28, 2015, transcript, p. 3.

6. Rob Nelson, personal interview, April 28, 2015, transcript, p. 8.

7. Rachel Abrams, "A Hunt to Find the Next Generation of Financial Advisors," *DealBook* (blog), *New York Times,* June 24, 2014, http://dealbook.nytimes.com/2014/06/24/a-hunt-to-find-the-next-generation-of-financial-planners/?_r=1.

8. Mark Miller, "Wanted: Financial Advisors Who Aren't about to Hang It Up," *Reuters,* February 20, 2014, www.reuters.com/article/2014/02/20/us-column-miller-finan-cialadvisers-idUSBREA1J1N920140220.

9. Ibid.

10. Paul Pagnato, personal interview, March 23, 2015, transcript, p. 5.

11. Ibid.

12. Ibid.

CHAPTER 5

Lone Ranger to Leader™

As the advising profession has moved from a focus on sales to technical expertise to wealth management partnership, the kind of firms that the most successful advisors build is changing, too. Today, it's no longer about running a one-person operation; now it's all about team. In fact, according to Fidelity Investments, 84 percent of high-performing advisors work in a team configuration versus only 48 percent of other advisors.[1]

Why the need for team? As the advising profession moves from offering a single product or service to providing whole wealth management, advisors can't go it alone anymore. There are now too many pieces of wealth management for one person to have the time or expertise to manage them all: financial planning, investing, banking, taxes, life insurance, estate planning, and more. Then, layer onto that a more sophisticated advising profession than ever before, involving the need for rainmaking, relational skills, technical skills, service skills, marketing skills, and so on . . . and you need a team to thrive.

In addition, if the client, the client's family, and the heirs to the client's wealth are going to be able to depend on an advisor, then advisors are going to have to build something that's truly going to outlast them, and that begins with a team. Having a strong team in place helps advisors operate out of integrity and avoid telling the big, fat lie that they will always be there for the client when they can't actually deliver.

Unfortunately, some advisors are still operating as sole practitioners, whether in practice or in principle. Some have stubbornly remained sole advisor in their firms, avoiding the hassle of taking on new advisors. Others who do have a team often keep the team members in the background when it comes to client relations, creating a bottleneck that puts too much pressure on the advisor and compromises the organization. It's another case of advisors framing themselves in an outdated way that is detrimental to their business: the old frame of "I am the best at serving my clients" versus the new frame used by the best in the business, "My team is the best at serving our clients." At ClientWise, we refer to this as framing oneself as a lone ranger (old frame) versus as a leader (new frame).

What's a lone ranger? Lone rangers do much of the work themselves. Lone rangers have chosen not to build team or, if they have a group of people working for them, the team may not operate as effectively as it could. Lone rangers believe they are the only one who can advise the client.

Working as a lone ranger can be exciting and rewarding. Yet it can be difficult and exhausting, too, especially when trying to sustain production and grow the business to higher levels. Yes, you can work harder and longer, but you're still likely to hit a limit with how far you can grow the business alone or without a true team.

If you believe, as emphasized earlier in this book, that the way of the future really is comprehensive wealth management—and if you believe that the client deserves more, today and in the future— then you've got to get other team members on board. This reframe is of value to you, the advisor, too. It frees you to focus on the work you love doing the most, it ensures that you can step away from the business when needed, and it gives you an advantage over competitors. The team reframe creates a win–win situation for advisor and client alike.

KEY CONCEPT

Going it alone is a tempting path, given its straightforward nature, but becoming a team leader expands your business opportunities: in the array of services you can offer your clients, in the number of clients you can take on, and in the length of time you can truthfully promise to serve your clients.

Where are you on the journey from lone ranger to leader? This chapter will help you explore this question and give you tools to improve your leadership skills and team performance, wherever you are on the lone-ranger-to-leader spectrum.

THE eXchange™

Online Tool 5.1: Leader's Journey Assessment

Take stock of where you are on the leadership journey by completing the brief, 15-item Leader's Journey Assessment on the eXchange™. This will help you identify your current areas of strength as a team leader versus opportunities for growth.

SURRENDER INDEPENDENCE TO INTERDEPENDENCE

The evolution from lone ranger to leader involves a major reframe. You must shift from framing yourself as the one and only—or the primary operator—of your business to framing yourself as the skilled leader of a competent team.

Advisors using the sales approach may tend to frame themselves as a lone ranger, as they are usually most comfortable in the trenches, where they can be sure of making the sale. But even those advisors who operate from a technical or wealth management approach can easily fall into the lone ranger mentality. In working with a client, they may take the "trust me" approach and make the relationship all about them, not about their team or even the client's participation and partnership.

In making themselves the primary person who interacts with, manages, and influences the client, these advisors are setting up potential disappointments in the future: disappointment if the advisor is unable to deliver everything promised due to lack of time and availability, if the advisor has blind spots on particular areas of wealth management that compromise chances of successfully meeting client goals, and/or if and when the advisor has to withdraw from the lead role of managing the client's wealth due to retirement, illness, or something else.

 KEY CONCEPT

Being a lone ranger means being vulnerable to external circumstances (e.g., illness, accident, having too many demands on your time) as well as internal ones (specialties you have not been trained in, areas in which you are unaware of your weaknesses). Creating a team of professionals circles the wagons, bulking up your coverage and thereby protecting both you and your clients.

The truth is that you have to let go to grow. For example, you may need to let go of the beliefs that

- the client service model has to be delivered by only you;
- you are the only one who can do a client review; or
- you possess all of the technical knowledge associated with delivering wealth management and that you can be the relationship manager, technician, rainmaker, operations person, and administrative manager.

These are some of the universal beliefs that lone rangers may need to let go of to become a leader.

Then there are those pieces that lone rangers will need to let go of that are unique to their particular firm, due to varying skill sets, strengths, client needs, and so forth. Regardless of the unique profile of a given firm and situation, the advisor undoubtedly will need to be willing to hand certain functions and responsibilities over to others on the team so the firm can offer true wealth management.

Another way to describe this is as surrendering independence to interdependence: letting go of the idea that you need to do everything yourself and replacing it with the notion that your job is to lead others in working as a team to get everything done for the client and the business. It's a reframe from rainmaker to CEO, from lone ranger to leader. When you're a salesperson working by yourself, you're "eating what you kill," so to speak. When you're a leader or a CEO, you've got to find the ability to let go and trust that in building this team, the profits will not only come but increase because you will be able to better serve the client.

COACHING CORNER

Regardless of whether you have a team, in what ways do you think you may still be operating as a lone ranger? Take some time to think about the way you spend your time each day. What kinds of lone ranger activities are you involved in? What kinds of leadership activities are you engaged in? Where would you feel comfortable making adjustments to help make the reframe from lone ranger to leader?

Surrendering independence for interdependence is not easy. One of my high-performing lone ranger clients, Bill, was certainly resistant at first. Bill was bringing in $18 million a year in income because he had done such an effective job of figuring out how to manage people's investments. He had been doing such a good job, in fact, that people had been telling him his whole adult life of how great a job he was doing and that he should keep up the good work. He was a phenom and everyone wanted more of him, so he just kept doing more.

When I introduced the concept of building a true team around him, Bill was shocked. All of the feedback he had received for years said that he should keep working his professional magic and manage more and more investment portfolios. Now I was encouraging him to learn how to step back and give some control to a team of professionals that he would have to build around himself?

Bill expressed concern that the high performance he had been generating for years might drop if he was no longer doing the investing himself. His statement on the topic was along the lines of, "Why would I ever want to risk having mediocre performance for my clients? They're paying me to run their portfolios; I'm going to run their portfolios."

Interestingly, when pressed further on the point, Bill shared that he already had a team—after all, he had hired a bunch of people to process all of the work he generated. I explained to him that what he had was a work group, not a team, and that he could tell the difference between the two by asking what would happen if he was removed from the work equation. "So," I asked him, "what would happen if you ever got injured or sick?"

The whole tent of his operation would fold—and Bill knew it. So we worked together to build a true team around him: better utilizing current team members, hiring new ones, building a network of other professional advocates in the wider wealth management business, and fostering an effective team culture. Over time, clients began to be able to rely on other people rather than just Bill, and they got more services than Bill alone could provide.

It turned out that Bill's clients, while they valued his investment expertise and capability, also needed more from him. They needed a true partner to design wealth strategies that could help them live the lives they truly wished to live. Now Bill and his team can meet those needs, and, should anything happen to him, Bill's tent won't fold.

In the old days, when you sold one instrument, you could go it alone. In today's wealth management business, you've got to include other people. You may play the role of lead wealth management advisor, but the team will also have a service leader, a technical person, and more—not just the CPA and the attorney, but other technicians like the relocation specialist, the private equity firm, the business valuation person, the primary banker, or the tax return preparer. Then you will have your traditional team as well, to cover areas like marketing, business, development, technology, and compliance. Some of these folks will be on your internal team; others may be on your virtual team, depending on the kind of firm you would like to run and whatever is needed to serve the client. One thing is certain: A team is needed to deliver true wealth management.

 ## The Three Kinds of Advisors to Add to Your Team

The most effective teams have three advisor roles in common. Several additional roles can be filled by team members or consultants dedicated to providing support in other areas, but these three advisor roles are central to delivering on the promises you make to your clients.

Senior Lead Advisor: The senior lead advisor is dedicated primarily to rainmaking activities, consistently filling the pipeline by taking meetings with new potential clients and centers of influence and bringing them on board. The secondary role of the senior lead advisor is as a strategic relationship manager, who only gets involved with clients when they need a more senior partner to help make a crucial decision. If a client is especially important to your team's success or a situation necessitates a higher level of care, the senior lead advisor might be brought in to partner with these clients in achieving their financial goals.

Lead Advisor: The lead advisor's primary role is relationship manager. Focused on complete client care, the lead advisor ensures that no accounts are leaving and that the team is delivering on the promises made to the client. The lead advisor also has a secondary set of four crucial responsibilities: (1) uncovering new assets from existing clientele, (2) finding new revenue opportunities to service existing clients more effectively, (3) connecting to the heirs of your clients' wealth and knowing when and where that wealth is ready to transition, and (4) building Loyal Client Advocates™ by engaging client relationships on a deeper level to uncover the potential clients within their networks.

Service Advisor: The service advisor takes care of all follow-through and follow-up. He or she is essentially responsible for completing the work promised to the client, so sometimes the service advisor is front and center with clients and other times he or she is behind the scenes, making sure all client information and paperwork is complete and in order. In addition, these service advisors will move into lead advisor and senior lead advisor roles according to your succession plan needs. You want your clients to be as comfortable with them as possible, and the longevity of their involvement will help with this.

The benefit of a team is that it allows you to home in on core competencies and the unique value you bring to the team with increased focus and efficiency. This won't be possible if you or any of your team members are wearing "all the hats," or trying to play the roles of senior lead advisor and lead advisor simultaneously. While you may work together to accomplish some of these responsibilities, only one team member is the driver of each.

TEAM DEFINED

For those advisors who do have teams today but who find that their teams are not operating at top capacity, the root of the problem may be found by looking at the way the team originally formed. In the beginning, when an advisor got started in the business, in any channel, the advisor was responsible for doing it all. The more successful the advisor became, the more he or she needed extra people to support the work. The result? The advisor hired staff members and created a "team."

Over time, the advisor became even more successful and therefore needed to hire more staff members, further growing the "team." The cycle continued until the advisor woke up one day to realize he or she had become a manager with a lot of mouths to feed on the so-called team.

Managing the team took lots of time and was not particularly enjoyable. What's more, the advisor never empowered the team members to create strong relationships with the client, so the client still depended on the advisor in spite of there being a team. More and more of the advisor's time got eaten up by the team instead of being freed up by it.

What happened in these situations? Instead of building an interdependent team that was able to make the advisor's life easier, the advisor built a work group that took lots of care and feeding. It's a common mistake that ends with the same results: The work group and the client remain dependent on the advisor because he or she did not follow the steps necessary to create an interdependent team empowered to build relationships with the client, and the advisor becomes overtaxed and overburdened as responsibilities grow rather than diminish. No wonder some advisors shudder at the idea of creating a team, while others run "teams" that are not nearly as productive and helpful to the advisor as they could be.

At ClientWise, we define *team* in the following way:

> A true team is a group of people who are fully committed
> to mutually defined and extraordinary success of the group
> as a unit and who hold themselves accountable for the
> achievement of that success as well as the methods by
> which that success is achieved.

A team is a group of people who are committed to joint success, a success that is extraordinary. How does one define *extraordinary*? The team gets to decide. For a true team to exist, all of the members need to have an opportunity to help define success. That's a little uncomfortable for the high-performing lone ranger used to calling the shots and trusting his or her own judgment. It calls the lone ranger to stretch out of his or her comfort zone. But remember, too, that the lone ranger is becoming a leader, and leaders have the privileged position of helping the group set the vision; the leader has an essential role in defining what success looks like for the team.

KEY CONCEPT

A team is not simply a group of people working on a project. The members of a true team are committed to achieving a shared goal. Everyone on the team agrees on what the goal entails, and everyone on the team contributes their skills and dedication while holding their fellow team members accountable for their contributions, leading to extraordinary success.

Team Accountability

A team is responsible for holding its members *accountable for the achievement* of their extraordinary, mutually defined success. The team members also hold each other *accountable for the methods* they use to achieve that success. So, as the journey toward success is undertaken, team members tune in to how the rest of the team is executing to get to that success. They hold one another accountable to getting stuff done and doing it in the best way. In addition, it's not a case of success at any cost but rather coming by success honestly and with integrity.

Let's look at that word *accountability*. In a financial sense, accountability is responsibility for the way that money is used and managed. In a governance sense, accountability refers to the liability or blameworthiness of a nonprofit or corporate entity in a given situation or general fashion. In a team sense, accountability involves holding others responsible, but the blame component is removed altogether.

The kind of accountability I am referring to here, with a true team, is a more expansive and collaborative experience. We're not talking oversight boards or authoritarian rule. We're talking team meetings, goal setting, and regular check-ins. It is about the magic that comes from being present, engaged, and aware of what each team member has agreed to contribute and work toward and staying in conversation to support the execution of the plan. On a true team, there is a grassroots culture of positive accountability. Supportive questions like "Hey, how's it going with Project X?" and "Is there anything you want to talk through on Y?" bubble up authentically and organically.

KEY CONCEPT

Accountability does not mean blame. On true teams, accountability is collaborative: Team members check with each other to make sure everyone is present, engaged, aware, supported, and on the path to executing the group's plan.

 Five Ways to Win Your Clients Over to the Team Reframe

At first, some clients may not feel comfortable letting their lone ranger advisors reframe themselves into leaders. Clients may trust the single advisor but may not yet have faith in the rest of the team—whether the team was formerly kept in the background or is altogether new. If this is the reality, the advisor may have to make a case to clients for why the transformation from lone ranger to leader is in the clients' best interest. Here are five ways to win clients over to the team idea. Remember: The most important part of this process is engaging the client and helping make him or her part of the lone-ranger-to-leader transformation.

1. Set up a meeting (ideally in person) with the client to let him or her know personally that you are cultivating your existing team or a new team to better serve the client.

2. Share the ways in which you are hopeful that the team will be able to better serve the client (e.g., be able to offer new

services across the wealth management spectrum, ensure that someone is always there for the client if you ever get sick or need to step away; provide a more robust team up and down the advisory chain to ensure quality of service; free you up to be there for the client during the big, strategic decisions; serve the client's heirs with advisors of varying ages and a succession plan in place; etc.).

3. Give the client a brief overview of the roles of each existing and new team member and share two or three strengths of that team member.

4. Ask the client what concerns he or she may have regarding the transition to a team approach; listen to the responses and validate the client's perspective ("I appreciate your concerns and look forward to working through them together. As our client, you always come first, and if you are not happy with the team, we want to know about it so we can continue to develop the team in a way that best supports you").

5. Ask for permission from the client to check in regularly to gather feedback on how the team is doing to make improvements and continue to develop them—and follow through.

It may be a process of education to help clients understand the value of the advisor shifting from the lone ranger approach to the team approach. Taking the time to speak personally with the client, outlining the benefits of the team approach, listening to client concerns, and circling back for team feedback can all make for a smoother and more successful transition.

The Old Team Structure versus the New Team Structure

The team reframe is not just about moving from being a lone ranger to leader of a team: It is also about moving from the old style to the new style of teaming. Teams of the past were built on a structure that put the advisor at the center of the group dynamic as a sort of gatekeeper between staff members and clients (as reflected in Figure 5.1). This put the advisor in a position of power, but it also created many

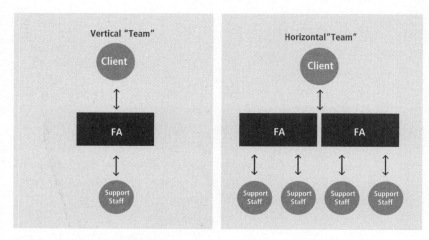

Figure 5.1 Old Team Structures

opportunities for the advisor to become a bottleneck as the bulk of what the client needed passed directly through the advisor; similarly, the bulk of the staff's work was also passed through the advisor on its way to the client.

As it turns out, the old form of a team wasn't really a team at all. If you removed the advisor, the team would implode because the client had the relationship with the advisor, not anyone else on the team. The advisor was "the man" or "the woman" to deal with on all issues. Sure, the client might be served by the staff in some ways, but the client did not view them as professional advisors. To create true interdependence, you've got to get other professionals working with the client.

Enter the new team structure, which places the client at the center of the group dynamic. As shown in Figure 5.2, the work flow travels directly from each team member to the client as well as through the team itself.

The new team structure removes the challenge of advisor bottlenecks, builds trust between the client and all team members, and encourages collaboration among team members. Information and work flow easily and efficiently from those with expertise and ownership in a given area to the client or through the team first when team input is needed.

Figure 5.2 New Team Structure

KEY CONCEPT

Traditionally, the client interacted solely with the advisor, who intentionally acted as a gatekeeper but inadvertently ended up being a bottleneck. To best serve clients, top teams now encourage interaction between the client and all of the members of the team, building trust between the client and the team and making all of the team's knowledge and skill available to the client.

THE eXchange™

Online Tool 5.2: A Guide to Defining Your High-Performing Team

Visit the eXchange™ for a 12-question guide to defining your unique high-performing team.

DO YOU HAVE A TEAM OR DO YOU HAVE A WORK GROUP?

Whenever I speak to advisors across the country about the need to have a team in place to deliver true wealth management, the responses vary. Some admit they have no team in place, others describe their team with confidence, and still others wonder if they are on the right track with their current team. I like to ask advisors in the last two situations to consider whether they have a true team or, instead, a work group.

A work group is made up of staff members and/or contractors to whom the advisor hands off work. Each member of the work group has individual goals that the advisor has set, but the group has not come together as a whole to mutually define success. Work group members may or may not happen to interact with each other, and they are not charged with keeping each other accountable.

You know you have a work group if

- you've hired a bunch of "staff" to work on individual projects, tasks, or roles, but you have not brought these individuals together to coalesce as a group with a common vision for success;
- you have defined what success means for the group without taking their input;
- you have resisted adding smart, intelligent technicians and relationship managers to the group in lieu of "worker bees"; and
- you hand off service work to the team but not relational work.

You know you have a work group when you eliminate the founder and the entire business implodes because the client is not accustomed to dealing with anyone but the founder. The founder is not so unlike a pole in a circus tent. Pull the pole down and what happens to the tent? It collapses.

KEY CONCEPT

If the members of your "team" work completely independently, do not share goals, do not interact, and do not help hold each other accountable, you have a work group, not a team. Consider implementing a true team structure to boost your team's performance and results.

In contrast, you know you have a true team when the client believes he or she is being served by the whole group rather than just the leader. If asked, the client would express that the team brings him or her more value than if the client worked with the lead advisor alone. In addition, you know you have a team when

- you observe members at a meeting and see every individual having a voice, speaking up, and taking a leadership role;
- day-to-day, you see team members acting as owners of their share of the business;
- you see team members working together, treating each other with respect, and supporting each other; and
- you sense a culture of inclusivity, collaboration, and camaraderie.

Last, if you have a true team, the members will believe the work that they are doing is contributing to team success for the benefit of the client. They will find their work joyful and will feel they are operating at their best.

 COACHING CORNER

Take some time to think about the group of people that are supporting you and your business. Is it a team or a work group? How do you know?

 Ten Tips for Fostering Team Behavior and Creating Sustainability and Success

1. Encourage storytelling, reminiscing, and anecdote sharing at team meetings. This can be focused on personal experiences related to key team goals and projects as well as personal experiences unrelated to work.

2. Find opportunities to talk with team members on an impromptu face-to-face basis to connect and share.

3. Create regular team social events and, on occasion, include family.

(Continued)

(Continued)

4. Create opportunities to share individual team members' feelings about the team's common intent and purpose, team goals, and ambience.

5. Create powerful team meetings that will be opportunities for the entire team to do real work together.

6. Consider the habit of "working together frequently" as a discussion topic for a team meeting. There will be more ownership if everyone is involved in the discussion and has agreed to actions.

7. Reinforce and talk about the team's shared goals whenever possible.

8. Actively identify where collective thinking or collective work should be used and would be more powerful than individual thinking and work (e.g., planning for the future, solving problems, and creating new approaches).

9. If team members are in the same office, minimize use of e-mail; drop in to see people face-to-face. If team members are not in the same office, encourage more use of the telephone, conference calls, and Skype versus e-mail.

10. Give feedback regularly. Be specific, be timely, and offer praise publicly.

CONCLUSION

Like it or not, as a professional in the financial services industry, you've been framed. Because you (or your predecessors) originally entered this business by selling a financial product, clients tend to view you as a salesperson. Most of them don't know that you've moved on from advising on a single product to offering more options. Although clients would love to work with a partner, many of them don't realize that you can be that to them—or already are—because, quite frankly, you may not have taken the time to educate them on your evolved role as a financial or wealth management advisor. Your job title may reflect the change, but busy clients may still be clueless.

I hope you are now a believer. If you agree that you are no longer a salesperson, you're a partner; if you're no longer interested in telling people you will always be there for them when in fact you don't have a succession plan in place; and if you are ready to trade the lone ranger mentality for the leader mentality, it's time to turn to Part II of this book, where you can begin to do the real work of reframing yourself, your team, and your business.

First, you get to have a conversation with your clients to gather input and learn about how they are framing you; then, you will have a chance to spend time with your team identifying how you would actually like to be framed. In the process, you will get to answer questions like, What kind of executive do you want to be? What kind of team do you want to build? And what do you want that team to be known for?

These are exciting times. No longer are you limited to advising on a single product. You don't have to sell; you can partner. What's more, you get to be the designer of your business, making conscious choices about what kind of clients you'd like to work with and the kind of services you are inspired to provide to these clients.

You no longer have to do it all, either, nor should you. You can build or develop your team to play key roles in serving the client so you are freed up to focus on the parts of the business you love, however you define them. There are a range of professionals out there for you to bring on, too, as part of your team, to support the client where you may not do so internally.

It's an opportunity for you to lead not just your team and your business but the industry, too. By reaching out to other financial professionals and taking them on as team members rather than mere referral sources, you set a new standard of collegiality in the industry and create a model of true wealth management for the client—one where the client is taken care of in all regards. That's noble!

NOTE

1. Fidelity Investments, *Plan, Diversify, and Differentiate: Three Strategies of High-Performing Advisors*, 2014, accessed May 31, 2015, https://nationalfinancial.fidelity.com/app/literature/view?itemCode=9587275&renditionType=pdf.

PART II

Five Steps to Reframing Your Business

CHAPTER 6

Discovering Your Current Frame

The ClientWise Conversation™

So here we are in the twenty-first-century world of the financial services profession. As explored in Part I, no longer is the advisor's role to sell to the client; now it is to partner with the client. In a marketplace where a team is needed, no longer is it effective to operate with the mentality of a lone ranger rather than a leader. What's more, a transformation is well underway, with advisors moving from providing a single product or service to offering a total wealth management solution for clients.

Whether advisors choose to deliver all of the products and services related to their particular brand of wealth management or not, being relevant in the life of the ideal client, knowing who they serve, and designing a total solution to meet the needs of that client are paramount. Even if the advisor outsources the other products and services, designing a total solution for the client is part of what the future advisory relationship will be about; it's what will make the advisor and advisory team or firm relevant.

It is also time in the twenty-first century for advisors to review with their clients what kind of value they provide and how they do it. In today's consumer-friendly marketplace, where the client has ample access to information, opportunities galore to do it him- or herself, and plenty of choices of whom to use as a provider of financial services, the advisor no longer has the liberty of simply deciding what he or she wants to provide the client. The wise advisor invites clients into the process of defining what is of value to them.

Not that it's all drudgery and obligation—along the way, the advisor has the freedom to refine the value the client needs so it matches the advisor's passions and strengths. In some cases, the advisor may seek out a new, better-matched target-client base if the gap between what the client wants and the advisor can deliver is large, or the advisor may build out a team to address gaps. In any case, the conversation must always begin with the client; from there, the advisor can shape this newly gained understanding to create a firm that can serve the right people in the right way.

Last, today's successful advisors take the long view. Not only do they promise their clients that they will always be there for them and their families, but they also build practices that can deliver on that promise. They work with their clients to involve their heirs in the wealth management process; they build diverse teams that can appeal to clients of different age groups. They develop trust between their clients and their teams, so everyone knows what to do if the lead advisor has to step away for a time due to illness, need for respite, or something else. These advisors have a real, live succession plan in place, evidenced by the way they are developing their team and strengthening clients' relationships with the team over time. These are, in essence, the five big reframes that successful advisors of today are engaging in (see Part I for more information).

KEY CONCEPT

The conversation about your role as a financial advisor, how you are framed, and the services you do and should offer must always—always!—begin with the client.

Figure 6.1 The Five Steps to Reframing Your Wealth Management Business

Any one of these reframes—as well as the unique reframes that a given advisor would like to make in terms of what clientele the advisor serves and how—involves a process. Reframing does not happen overnight, and it does not happen without engaging in specific action. Five specific steps to reframing (shown in Figure 6.1) will help you get the results you desire.

Step 1: Collect data. Before you can reframe your wealth management practice, you first need to understand how you are being framed. To do so, you'll be going right to your clients to find out how they frame you today. That's step 1, collecting information about your current frame. This is the step that we'll explore in this chapter.

Step 2: Define frame. Next, it's time to "go within" your firm and/or your team and engage in the process of envisioning what your new frame will be. That's step 2 of the reframing process: defining the new frame. Here you will be asking and answering, "How do you want your clients to frame you in the future?"

This process will involve looking at the kind of value you'd like to provide versus the kind of value that your clients are seeking. If there is a gap, this process will involve resolving the discrepancy, whether to tweak the kind of services you offer to meet the needs of your current client list, to build out a team to meet those needs, or to outline a new ideal client list to match your own strengths and interests as an advisor.

Step 3: Build frame. After you define what new frame you want to be seen through, you will be ready to build the new frame. This will involve a new frame for your team as well as a new frame for you as a leader. It will also entail creating new marketing assets that consistently portray your new frame. That's step 3: building the new frame.

Step 4: Renew relationships. Once the new frame is in place, it's time to go back to your clients and communicate the new frame by renewing relationships. Here, you will educate your clients on your new frame, including the new kind of wealth management you are set to deliver, its value to clients, and the way your team will be integral to its delivery. That's step 4: renewing relationships.

Step 5: Create advocates. Last, to help the new frame "stick" and to encourage the growth of your firm, you will spend time creating advocates for your firm. Some will be clients, some will be other professionals, but all will understand the new frame and be able to communicate it consistently to others. That's step 5: creating advocates who are willing to accurately frame you while making introductions between you and potential new clients.

When followed with integrity, these five steps will help you reframe your practice so that it becomes the most effective version of itself, one with clear value that clients desire and that you and your team enjoy providing.

 KEY CONCEPT

Reframing your wealth management business involves five important steps: collecting information on your current frame, defining your new frame, building your new frame, renewing relationships, and creating advocates.

Now that we've taken a high-level look at the five-step process for reframing your wealth management business, we will spend the rest of the chapter drilling down into step 1 so you can master it.

Who Are You Reframing For?

Like it or not, you've been framed! The truth is that everybody frames you, so everybody eventually needs to learn about your reframe. Sometimes it is your client who is framing you, but sometimes it is your own team. Similarly, the professionals who refer you work and to whom you refer work probably have a frame for you as well.

All of these audiences not only would benefit from experiencing your reframe, but they also must learn about your new reframe for it to be truly effective. The reframe can only work if you are consistent with the message you deliver across audiences.

Because you are constantly learning and the industry is ever changing, your firm will (or should) always evolve, too. Therefore, by extension, parts of your frame likely will always be changing. After all, to thrive in financial services, you will always need to be innovating, creating capacity, adding new capabilities and human capital, creating new processes, adding and changing new services . . . whew! This list seems endless. I'm sure you get the point.

It's important to recognize that you will always need to be thinking about how you're being framed, how you and your firm want to be framed, and what you consistently need to be doing to make sure there is a clear alignment with how you're being framed and how you want to be framed as a leader, a team, and a firm! Isn't nice to know that you now have a process for how to do this, now and in the future?

You'll likely revisit this process for many years to come. I invite you to edit it, adjust it, and make it your own. Let me know how it's working for you. Join our community to get help from others who are also leading a reframing process, hear their stories, and share your own. After all, that's what our ClientWise™ community is all about.

No matter which audience you'd like to reframe yourself for, the reframing process outlined in this part of the book will work. For example, although this chapter focuses on using step 1 of the reframing process with clients, you can just as easily use this step with other professionals to whom you send and from whom you receive work. Simply substitute the word *professional* for *client* as you read through the passage and you will have the guidance you need to interview other professionals. (Note: We recommend that you interview the professionals you work most closely with.)

THE CLIENTWISE CONVERSATION™

The first step of the reframing process is to have a conversation with your clients, as well as with professionals with whom you work, to better understand how they frame you: how they perceive you, your services, your team, and your firm (see Figure 6.2).

I suggest using a very clear script and set of talking points for how this conversation should run, which my firm developed in 2006 and has been road-testing ever since, with more than 50,000 advisors having completed this process (and you may be one of them).

The ultimate goal with this conversation, which we call the Client-Wise Conversation™, is to collect data from the marketplace today so you can look for patterns and get a clear picture of how you are being framed . . . or mis-framed, as the case may actually be.

For example, do your clients see you as selling insurance without realizing that you also provide guidance on building an investment portfolio? Do your clients perceive you as old school, even though you now have advisors on staff who are from the millennial generation? Do your clients think you operate solo when, in fact, you have a team? Chances are that as you discover how clients frame you, you will also discover that to some degree they mis-frame you, meaning that there is a gap between the value they understand you to provide and the kind of value you actually provide.

You need to know why your clients mis-frame you so that you know where a reeducation process may need to take place during the reframe process. For example, your clients may need to be informed that you do more than sell insurance, that you have advisors with whom their heirs may be more comfortable speaking, and that you have a team in place should you ever need to step away due to family illness or any other eventuality.

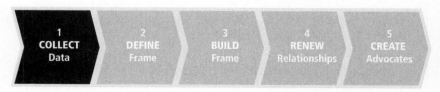

Figure 6.2 Reframe Step 1: Collect Data from the Marketplace

Getting a read on the client's frame for you will also provide you with feedback on how well you are currently doing with framing your business. It gives you a baseline of your current "frame job." It will let you know if the conversations you've been having with clients have been effective, if your marketing material is clear and accurate, and if those who send you new business have been framing you the right way.

It's altogether possible that you will discover that you have been doing a great job framing yourself, in which case you can simply plan to build from here during steps 2 and 3 of the reframing process—define and build. Alternatively, you might discover small discrepancies, or you might be surprised to discover big gaps between the ways you'd like to be seen by clients and the ways they appear to actually see you. Regardless of the outcome, you will have more clarity on how accurately your clients frame you today so that you have the data you need to move forward with the reframe process.

KEY CONCEPT

Because your clients are perhaps the most important asset your firm holds today, the first step of the reframing process is to have a conversation with your clients, as well as with professionals with whom you work, to better understand how they frame you—that is, how they perceive you, your services, your team, and your firm.

INDUSTRY INSIGHT: WISE CLIENTS, WISE ADVISOR

As Tom Weilert of Weilert Wunderlick Armstrong in Dallas would admit, he didn't believe he had the time to conduct the ClientWise Conversation™ with clients—yet as soon as he had completed the first five interviews, he realized that he needed to make time. Tom has now interviewed nearly every one of his clients because he realizes how much he can learn from them, and his business has benefited greatly.

For the first 30 years of Weilert's career, he was accurately framed as an insurance specialist. When he and his partners decided that they were going to expand their firm to offer holistic retirement-income distribution planning that incorporated multigenerational estate planning, they knew that the massive change would require additional team members and, perhaps more important, a reframe. Enter the Client-Wise Conversation™.

Weilert started his ClientWise Conversations™ close to home. His first interviews were with in-house staff and close professional associates. What he found in the process was that although he already had the trust of his staff and network of professionals, the descriptions they gave of the services his business provided were completely inconsistent. He needed to take charge of his frame.

As the transitions to the business came and the conversations with clients began and continued, the benefits of this open communication shone through. "What the ClientWise Conversation™ did was help us frame our own firm up in our own mind," says Weilert. Knowing how clients saw them helped to direct the efforts of Weilert and his partners. "What the ClientWise Conversation™ forced us to do was to find ourselves. Once we had a definition of who we were, then we could begin to educate the client."[1]

The transition from insurance to retirement-income distribution planning took time and many, many conversations. With each new round of feedback came new ideas for the firm and new promises to make and keep. Some clients weren't able to re-frame the firm in their minds, sticking with the old frame of insurance specialist, but others were thrilled with the new services, and additional clients came aboard.

Today, Weilert Wunderlick Armstrong has a clear vision of itself, a wide client base, a strong value statement, a four-characteristic definition of an ideal client, 16 diverse areas taken into consideration while planning distributions, and a partner structure that ensures the firm will be around to follow through on their promise of multigenerational wealth and risk management. And to think, this all started with a (ClientWise) conversation.

It's time to have a conversation with your clients to discover how they are framing you. At ClientWise, we have developed a set of five specific questions that together form the ClientWise Conversation™; these questions will help you collect the feedback you need to move forward with the framing process. In fact, we strongly urge you to use these exact questions, in this exact order. We have tested them with well over 50,000 advisors and have made adjustments along the way so that you don't have to. The five questions are as follows:

1. What is the one thing you value most about how my firm and I serve you?

2. What is the one thing you would most like me to change or improve about my firm and how I serve you?

3. If you were to describe the services that my firm and I offer you, to clients like yourself, what would you say?

4. If you were to describe what we've achieved together for as long as we've worked together, what would you say?

5. Among your other professional advisors in your life, who do you trust the most and why?

Each and every one of these questions is included for a reason, which we will explore in the remainder of the chapter. But let's start with some guidance on how best to set up the meeting.

 ## The ClientWise Conversation™: Who, When, and Where?

Who? You may be wondering who should be interviewing clients and professionals and gathering information. In general, I like to recommend that the advisor conduct these conversations because it is an opportunity for you to continue to build trust directly with the client and to demonstrate your very real commitment to the framing process. There is also a personal touch that only you can give as the advisor.

That being said, there may be times where the situation calls for someone else to conduct the interviews. Perhaps you feel that someone on your team has the right people skills to do the most effective job, such as your HR director, your chief marketing officer, or a registered assistant who has interacted with the client a great deal.

Alternatively, you may have a relationship with a consulting or coaching firm that you trust and feel would do an excellent job interfacing with clients on your behalf. This can be helpful in cases where you feel the clients would be able to be more open and honest with their input if they are able to speak to someone with a bit of distance from you.

When? As for when to conduct the ClientWise Conversation™, I strongly recommend that you schedule it as its own conversation rather

(*Continued*)

(*Continued*)

than trying to tag it onto the end of normal client review. Many advisors will try to maximize their time by dumping this interview at the back end of a client review. That's totally understandable, and yet it isn't really ideal for getting the most out of the conversation.

If, in the end, you feel that you must conduct the ClientWise Conversation™ at the end of a client review, there is a way to do it that will serve you best. When you set the appointment for the client review, ask the client for permission to add the ClientWise Conversation™ to the agenda. Then, at the start of the meeting, check in again to request permission and make sure the client is still okay with this piece of the agenda.

When the client review is complete and the client expresses satisfaction with it, ask permission to move into the ClientWise Conversation™. If the client agrees, take a break to reset the room: Open the door, get a cup of coffee, head to the bathroom. When the client returns to the room, he or she will bring greater openness than would have occurred without the break.

Where? At ClientWise, our research and the experiences shared with us by our coaching clients indicate that this model is most powerful when used in a face-to-face conversation. These have a much more personal touch and people tend to linger in them longer, so you have more time with a client and can gather far more information than is generally possible by phone. Therefore, we strongly recommend this approach whenever possible.

THE eXchange™

Online Tool 6.1: Checklist for Conducting the ClientWise Conversation™ after a Client Review

For a how-to checklist on conducting the ClientWise Conversation™ successfully at the end of a client review, if a separate meeting is not possible, visit the eXchange™.

KEY CONCEPT

There are three different entities that can conduct the ClientWise Conversation™: You as the advisor may conduct it yourself, you may choose to have someone on your team conduct the conversation with the client, or you may hire a consultant to facilitate the conversation.

THE MEETING SETUP

Before you get into the logistics of setting up the ClientWise Conversation™, ask yourself, are you willing to do this work? The best and the brightest in the business, those who are really ambitious and courageous and want to grow and deliver top-drawer services for their clients, find the time to have these conversations. If you want to move to that proverbial next level, then you have to want to do this work, too. You're going to need to carve out time in your schedule to invite others to the meeting and, most important, to conduct the actual conversation.

As you think about the time commitment, plan on interviewing 20 to 25 clients for a period of 20 to 30 minutes each. Not five to 10, but 20 to 25. There's a good reason for this: It helps to have time to practice and warm up. With the first five people you speak to, you may find yourself struggling to remember the questions. The next five, you may get the questions right but may not capture the answers in the most helpful way. By the next five, you are likely to get into a groove and then be able—with the next five to 10—to really start to hear specific patterns of feedback.

As you prepare to engage in the ClientWise Conversation™, another question to ask yourself is whether you are open to having conversations with clients that will allow you to improve your own sense of self-awareness. Feedback is only meaningful if you are able to hear it from an open and nondefensive perspective. Take some time to think about whether you are ready to be open-minded in this process and genuinely interested in hearing your clients' responses. If fear or disinterest comes up, consider talking to a coach certified by the International Coach Federation who can help you sort through those responses and clear your mind to be open to the results.

When you are feeling motivated and open to feedback, it's time to start teeing up meetings with your clients. Plan to start with whomever you would consider to be the five easiest clients for you to have this kind of conversation with. They should also be clients whose opinions you respect and who can provide you with honest input.

Before you pick up the phone to invite clients to set up a date and time to have the in-person ClientWise Conversation™, be sure to prepare for even this introductory call. Think about the client and the relationship you have built with him or her. Think about the kinds of conversations you've had with this client over the years when he or she has provided you with feedback. Bring a sense of understanding of the client and a sincere appreciation for what you have built together into the call. The client will sense it in your voice, and you will be prepared to connect with the client on issues relevant to the client's wealth, life goals, career goals, friends, and family as you've regrounded yourself in your past work together.

So let's talk about the setup. First, schedule an appointment for the in-person meeting. When you make the phone call to each client, explain that you want to ask for an appointment to get some input about how you are serving them.

In particular, explain

- that you are looking for ways to improve your practice
- because your business is growing and
- that you're calling a select few clients
- whose opinions you respect a great deal, like theirs,
- and would it be possible for them to meet with you in person within a reasonable time frame, such as the next week or two, for 20 to 25 minutes,
- so you can get some feedback on what's working, what's not working, and what could be done to improve their experience with your firm.

With a lead-in like that, how can your client say anything but yes?

Once your client has agreed to meet with you and you both have the conversation on the calendar, you'll need to prepare for the appointment. Begin by identifying what you genuinely appreciate about the client: not one thing you appreciate, but three things you appreciate, as you're going to share these at the in-person meeting.

Next, see if you can answer the five questions on the client's behalf before even having the meeting. What do you think he or she will say to each of the questions? Then, be prepared for the possibility that the client may share much more (or less) than you might have thought.

Perhaps there are other questions that are important to you, too, such as how important the client believes it is to be connecting to the heirs of his or her wealth; how comfortable he or she is with the other members of the team; how the client would describe wealth management; how confident, on a scale of 1 to 5, 5 being the best, the client is in the plan to achieve the goals and outcomes for his or her wealth; and so on. If so, add them to the end of your script for the conversation, to be posed after the five questions have been asked.

Also, think about the types of "other trusted advisors" your client might be working with (e.g., accountant, banker, realtor, etc.), as you'll be inquiring about this piece, too, and it helps to have some thoughts about what you want to know in case the client needs some clarification or prompting. In addition, rehearse your calls with someone. In fact, the first call to make when rehearsing could just start, "Hi, Mom . . ." You never know! Keep it light, friendly, and relaxed.

COACHING CORNER

With whom would you like to conduct the ClientWise Conversation™? Think about both clients and professionals whom you serve and know. When you are ready, make a list of 20 to 25 clients you'd like to speak with, and another list of the same number of professionals you'd like to speak with. The first five people you interview in either group should be those who are easiest for you to speak to and connect with. Schedule the more challenging interviews after that.

KEY CONCEPT

Be sure to prepare for the ClientWise Conversation™. Do this by opening your mind to hear and accept whatever feedback you may receive, calling clients to schedule an appointment for the conversation, blocking out your time for these conversations, figuring out what you appreciate about your clients, and rehearsing how the conversation will go.

 Five Steps to a Successful ClientWise Conversation™

1. Meet with the client in person rather than over the phone; it's more personal and gives the client time and space to provide more in-depth answers.

2. Make the meeting one on one, rather than showing up with three team members and risking intimidating the client.

3. Come from a position of strength, not weakness. Explain to the client that as your business continues to grow, you are always looking for ways to improve and better serve your clients.

4. Avoid becoming defensive; instead, let the client know that his or her insight is important to you, listen, and take notes to show you are taking the client seriously.

5. Use the five most important words early and often: "Tell me more about that."

Launching the Conversation: Questions 1 and 2

You've set up the meeting and now it is time to speak with your client, preferably in person and at a meeting that is separate from a client review. Before you dive into the questions, you can launch the meeting with some helpful techniques. At ClientWise, we ask all of our clients to begin the meeting by again stating its purpose. For example:

"Joe, I wanted to meet with you and ask you to help me think about the way I am running my practice. I value your opinion, and I would like to ask you for some honest feedback."

It's helpful to ground the client in the purpose of the meeting as this will be a new kind of conversation, probably unlike those you've had before. There will be no discussion of investments, financial planning, or the capital markets as you are meeting with the client to invite him or her to provide you with feedback about you and your practice. This opening comment will also build trust and rapport with your client as you express that you appreciate his or her feedback.

Remember, too, as you launch the conversation that you are coming from a position of strength. Your attitude is one of excitement and openness because your practice is doing well and you would like to do even better at serving clients in the ways they need. It's all part of a philosophy of continual improvement or lifelong learning.

The next step we ask all of our clients to take is to tell the person three things that you like or admire about him or her. For example:

"I have always appreciated how knowledgeable you are about what I do, and how thorough you are about doing your homework before we meet."

"I really appreciate how you always confirm our appointments and make sure it is convenient for me. That kind of sensitivity is unusual."

"I value the trust you put in me, especially the way you follow my advice when I make recommendations."

By telling the other person three things you like or admire about him or her, you are setting a positive tone for the meeting and further building trust. (Of course, these observations need to be authentic to be effective.) Recent research by a Japanese team has shown that not only do compliments serve as social rewards that have a positive effect on recipients not unlike that of money, but they also motivate people to perform better after receiving them.[2] You want your clients' help, and this is a great method to start paving the way to get it!

There are no right or wrong words to acknowledge your clients; simply offer them some evidence that you understand them and value specific things about them. In fact, having a perfect script is probably a mistake. Your acknowledgment should be tailored to the client you are talking to and personal to them. Authenticity and sincerity are the most important elements to this step.

KEY CONCEPT

Start your meeting on a positive note by giving your client three authentic compliments. When you build trust by showing you appreciate someone on an individual level, that person is inclined to return the favor, which will pave the way to a productive conversation.

With the meeting launched, you can begin asking the five Client-Wise Conversation™ questions, beginning with Question 1 and then moving on to Question 2. To be effective, the questions need to be asked in the order they are given. The reason for this lies in value. Often, it's easier for the clients to identify first what is working for them, what they value, and how they enjoy working with you today.

Most interviewers assume that the current setup is working well and thus want to skip that part of the interview in favor of getting to the question of what can be done better. If you take that approach, you'll likely hear from clients that the relationship is fine, they are happy, and they wouldn't change much. "Keep doing what you're doing," you'll be likely to hear.

This is not the feedback you are looking for! Instead, give clients the space to start thinking and talking about their experiences with you over the years, and this will warm them up to giving you the constructive feedback you are asking for.

Do not, under any circumstances, think that you can mail these questions out in some sort of written or typed survey. It's best if you do not even send them to the client in advance. I had one Morgan Stanley advisor in Chicago call me to specifically tell me the ClientWise Conversation™ didn't work. When I responded with some questions of my own to figure out why, I discovered that he had mass mailed the five questions to all 400 of his clients and got (surprise surprise!) very little response. You need the questions answered, and you need them answered truthfully, with your clients' authentic responses. These answers are best acquired in person.

Also important to note, the conversation will be richer than just the five questions with authentic answers by your clients. As your clients answer the five questions I have provided here, you will learn information that may raise additional questions for you. Plan to ask any follow-up questions that spring to mind and to be in the flow of the conversation. Remember, however, that in the first meeting, you must cover all five of the questions. Start with Question 1:

What is the one thing you value most about how my firm and I serve you?

This question allows you to begin the inquiry by gathering positive information, which is likely to put both you and the client at ease. Most people don't particularly enjoy giving negative or constructive feedback, whereas they are far more willing and/or comfortable saying something positive. So this is an icebreaker question. Of course, it's more than an icebreaker. At its heart, it is a means of determining how exactly the client perceives your value as a professional. You are gathering data to let you know how your clients are currently framing your business. What value do they think you provide them?

As with all of these questions, it's important to word them as they are shown here. The wording has been chosen expressly and tested across thousands of situations. In the case of Question 1, notice that the question doesn't ask, "What is the most important way that you feel my firm and I serve you?" It asks, "What is the one thing . . . ?" Neurolinguistics research shows that people tend to freeze up or struggle to answer a question about "the most important" something, whereas they answer "one thing" questions with greater ease and creativity.

The request to pull the superlative, tip-top, number one "most important thing" answer out of the air raises the blood pressure of the person trying to come up with a brilliant, insightful, unassailable response; in fact, psychology professor Barry Schwartz has called the quest to make the perfect choice "a recipe for misery."[3] Spare your clients the torture and stick with "one thing"! After all, they are likely to give you more than one thing anyway!

The Five Most Important Words

Regardless of how the client responds to your questions, the five most important words you will use during the ClientWise Conversation™ are these: "Tell me more about that." These are powerful words that will encourage your client to expand, to offer you even more data, and to share more deeply. This will give you an even clearer sense of how you are being framed. In addition, by showing a sense of interest and curiosity in your client's comments, you will also have a chance to build greater rapport with the client.

It's all about active listening, focusing your attention on the client through the words you use and the posture you hold. Active listening involves responding to a client's words with statements that encourage him or her to say more, such as "Expand upon that, please" or "What did you mean when you said ___?" With active listening, you will also take time to make sure you truly understand what it is that the client is trying to communicate to you. For example, you may repeat back to the client what you think you heard, and then ask, "Did I get that right?" inviting the client to confirm, clarify, or correct the meaning.

In addition, it will help you to be mindful of the different levels of communication that are really taking place during the conversation. At level 1 exist the words that the clients give you. Your job is to hear their words. This is about what the clients have to say, not what your thoughts and opinions are.

At level 2 is the meaning of the clients' words. What they are saying may mean something different to them than it does to you. Last, consider level 3 of the communication, that is, reading between the lines. What can you intuit by what your clients are saying to you? Try to listen at a really deep level, and check in with your clients to ensure that your intuition is correct. Don't be afraid to say, "I think I'm hearing you say something else" or "Let me see if I'm really understanding you" and then stating the message you think you are receiving. It is better to check in and be corrected than to not check in and proceed with making changes in your firm on the basis of a misunderstanding of client feedback.

After you have asked your client what is the one thing that he or she values most about your firm and you've taken time to listen and document the answer, it's time to ask Question 2:

What is the one thing you would most like me to change or improve about my firm and how I serve you?

With this question, you are moving on to gather information about how you can be a more effective partner to your clients. If the answer resonates and/or you discover a pattern across multiple clients, you can build this change into the reframe. Wow, is this question powerful! Who has better insight into how you can best serve the client than the client him- or herself? Your client is a treasure trove of useful information on how you can effectively reframe your business. As long as you are able to build trust during the conversation and maintain an open attitude rather than being defensive, you have the potential to learn some very useful information with this question.

In fact, one of my clients, an advisor from the Midwest, affiliated with one of the big brokerage houses, informed me that this question saved him from losing his biggest client. I picked up the phone one day to hear him share, "I just want you to know that you saved my career." I will admit that I was stunned. Truth be told, I had never met the man—let's call him Paul—but he had gone through one of our coaching programs and had learned the ClientWise Conversation™ from his ClientWise coach.

Paul explained the following: "My number one client, who is a chief executive of a major company, was about to leave me—until I asked him, 'What is the one thing I could change or improve?' His answer was, 'Stop calling my home number and leaving messages for me to call you back. Send me an e-mail, it would be preferred, and, oh, by the way, go set up an appointment and meet my wife. She really has no clue about the finances, and you need to educate her.'"

Why did Paul's client make these requests? Here's what was really happening. This client was the chief executive of an international company and found himself traveling all over the world. Paul would call the client for his periodic check-in because this client was an ultra-high-net-worth individual, and he had a very large investment portfolio. A trainer or consultant somewhere along the way had told Paul that this was the right thing to do, the "best practice."

But here's the thing: The client never asked for Paul to call him monthly and certainly not at his home number. Instead of this being a good thing for the client, it was causing him all sorts of headaches, because each time Paul would leave a voice mail on the home machine, the client's wife would think that something had gone wrong with the couple's investment portfolio, so she would call the husband in the middle of the night, say, Tokyo time, waking him up to ask, "Hey, by the way, the advisor just called and left this message. Is everything okay?"

The truth of the matter was that nothing was wrong at all, but Paul's "best practice" home number check-in caused all sorts of stress, disruption, and headaches for the client. The client was ready to dump his "annoying" advisor who just wouldn't let up with the monthly calls to his home phone—until his advisor took the time to gather feedback from him. Question 2 saved this advisor from losing his biggest client.

It saved him his career, too, because this client had referred over 50 clients to him who were all high-net-worth individuals and employees of the international firm that the client led. If the client had left the advisor, the rest of these clients would have departed, too.

Instead, this story has a fantastic ending. Instead of losing his client, Paul actually reframed his business and gained new clients by developing a whole education series to better educate the spouses of his clients. The ClientWise Conversation™ helped him realize that he was not connecting with half of his clients—the spouses—and he made a meaningful change in his value proposition as a result. In fact, it has become the centerpiece to his value proposition, as he primarily works with C-suite executives, many of whom are married and appreciate this piece of support.

This story makes you wonder what you will discover when you ask your clients about the one thing that they would most like you to change or improve about your firm and how it serves them, doesn't it?

 KEY CONCEPT

Asking clients what they value about your firm and what they would change about your services can result in new insights and new ideas for you, and more personalized services for your clients. Be sure to follow up client comments often with the request, "Tell me more about that."

Document, Document, Document

Another key aspect of the ClientWise Conversation™ is to document everything you are hearing the client share. Ask the client for permission to do so, with words like, "The insight and the words and phrases that you are sharing with me are really important. Do you mind if I take notes?"

Then, as you take notes, try to capture the client's words and phrases rather than simply paraphrasing. The reason is that words and phrases mean different things to different people. For example, when facilitating workshops, I often write the word TENDER up on the board and hear back from the group that it means so many different things to different people: chicken, steak, soft, small boat, Elvis ("Love Me Tender"). This is just one example of how words mean different things to different people. Try that out, by the way, at your next team meeting. Ask everyone at the same time what the word on the board means to them. It's always a laugh, but it makes the point that checking in about what words and phrases mean to different people really matters.

So, to ensure you are capturing your client's intended meaning, write down his or her words, not your own interpretation of them. As part of this process, also make absolutely sure that you understand what those words and phrases mean. Understanding precisely what the client means will ensure you gather useful data to consider later when constructing your new frame.

In the end, documenting the client's responses will help you later be able to look for patterns in the data that you collect because the patterns will give you all the insight that you need to have. Plan to put these notes in an Excel spreadsheet or other template that works for you so you can analyze it later.

 THE eXchange™

Online Tool 6.2: ClientWise Conversation™ Data Collector

Visit the eXchange™ for a note-taking template that you can use during the Client-Wise Conversation™ to capture your client's answers.

Question 3

When my firm first designed the questions in the ClientWise Conversation™ back in 2006, we made a mistake. There were only four questions at the time, not five, and that's because we didn't know that Question 3—the next one that you will use when conducting the ClientWise Conversation™—would not provide us with the kind of feedback we anticipated. Whoops! The question read as follows:

If you were to describe the services that my firm and I offer you, to clients like yourself, what would you say?

In Question 3, we were trying to get at the heart of what kind of services clients believed their advisors provided to them. That's fair enough, I think, with a question like this one. Yet, the answer that thousands of clients provided when asked this question was altogether different than the one we expected. Instead of saying things like, "You offer reasonably priced life insurance" or "You help clients build strong retirement portfolios," they said things like, "I trust you," "You take care of my family," "You've always been there for me," and "I can count on you."

The clients' answers had everything to do with building a trustful relationship. It had very little to do with answering the actual question, which invited people to describe the advisor's services—unless, of course, building a trusting relationship was the one most important thing that the advisor was providing to the client as a service.

Jonathan Beukelman, Managing Director of Wealth Management at the Beukelman Group,[4] discovered a similar reality early in his career and ultimately used it to help him frame himself for clients in a way that would be truly helpful to them. As a natural listener, Beukelman asked questions of his prospects and clients early on. In response, they told him the interesting truth that they didn't get particularly excited to hear about all the great investments his firm had told him to talk about to them.

What they really wanted was his support with the big questions, like how to pass their money down to their kids in the best way, how to educate their children about money, and how to make sure that they didn't ruin the next generation by not transitioning their wealth properly. This information helped Beukelman understand early on the value of the support relationship he could supply his clients. Most people need more than a mutual fund manager, Beukelman discovered—they need a financial advisor. What clients needed was not one piece, but the whole picture.

Over the years, when Beukelman has asked his clients what they need from him, they will often express concerns regarding their adult children. Beukelman doesn't shy away from talking directly to his clients' children, often when the kids are in their early twenties. Instead, he says lightheartedly, "Let me at them."

Over the course of his conversations with them, Beukelman has discovered that some of these kids "just need . . . patient conversation."[5] Instead of focusing on money management per se, Beukelman focuses on listening to these individuals and helping to keep a "fire in their gut" so they have the motivation to manage their money well, to "just go on and attack it."[6] Beukelman, whose firm specializes in managing family wealth, understands that the value of the advisor to the client is in the trusting relationship he and his team can provide, not in their ability to sell services to them.

We discovered the same reality as Beukelman when road-testing Question 3 of the ClientWise Conversation™: From the clients' view, the greatest value they receive from their advisor is to have a trusting relationship. In fact, this was the number one answer that was given when we asked clients, "If you were to describe the services that my firm and I offer you, to clients like yourself, what would you say?" We had learned something very important by asking Question 3. Clearly, though, we needed to add a different question to elicit the client's view on what kind of services the advisor offered. That's where Question 4 came in.

Yet, we did not remove Question 3 as we felt it was incredibly important to retain for two reasons. First, we believed that advisors needed to hear out loud from their clients how important the trusting relationship was to clients. Second, we knew that enabling the clients to enunciate for themselves that the trusting relationship was important to them would have a powerful impact on the clients. Both advisors and clients would gain a firsthand understanding, in the moment, of how much value the trusting relationship brings to clients, a value that could not be easily replicated by switching to another firm.

KEY CONCEPT

Asking clients to describe the services you provide usually reveals the most important asset in your relationship with the client: the trusting relationship itself.

▼ Avoid the Dance of Being Defensive

No matter what answers you get during the ClientWise Conversation™, you never want to fall into defending yourself or your firm. Instead of responding to the clients right on the spot with counter-comments to their points, focus instead on listening clearly, encouraging additional comments, and taking notes. Plan to remain singularly focused on gathering the data. Because you are not yet at the point where you know how you will want to reframe your business, stay in listening mode rather than speaking mode. You will have a chance to speak to the clients in a future conversation to address their concerns (step 4: renewing relationships). That conversation will take place when you are crystal clear on how you want to reframe yourself, your team, and/or your firm.

Question 4

Question 4 centers around achievement. It's a powerful question because it gets the clients to say in their own words what it is you have achieved together. It gets them to describe the value of your services out loud.

> If you were to describe what we've achieved together for as long as we've worked together, what would you say?

When the clients believe they have achieved something and they are able to articulate that something—when they own and know for themselves what they have achieved in partnership with you, the advisor—there is magic. The client makes a real connection in his or her mind between what you do as an advisor and why it is valuable to him or her.

Now if you as the advisor tell the client, "This is of value to you," the client won't believe it; it won't sink in or feel real or authentic. But if clients say out loud what is of value to them, it becomes real. Therein lies the genius of Question 4.

KEY CONCEPT

Asking the client about what the two of you have achieved together illuminates for you what is of value to the client, and illuminates for the client the value that you provide to him or her.

 Asking "What Have We Achieved Together?" During Client Reviews

I would argue that every single advisor needs to ask a client Question 4 on every single client review, not just during the ClientWise Conversation™. What's more, advisors need to get really smart about documenting what the client believes he or she has achieved in working with the advisor. There needs to be a memorialization of this value discussion after every client review. Send an e-mail; send a letter. "Really great that we were able to connect today to review the outcomes and goals that you have for your wealth and your life as it relates to your family. By the way, it was great to hear you say that we achieved X since we last met."

At the end of the year when there is an annual review, ask Question 4 and recap the things that the client believes were achieved over the course of a year; for example, "We've rebalanced investment portfolios, we've retitled life insurance policies, we've updated an estate plan, we've together made a decision about who would take care of the kids if something were to happen to Mom and Dad. We helped a child find the right college to go to, and we funded that second home. We provided a line of credit to buy that second business or to expand the business." These are all really powerful achievements.

Question 5

The last question that needs to be asked during the ClientWise Conversation™ is Question 5:

> Among your other professional advisors in your life, who do you trust the most and why?

There are two reasons that an advisor wants to ask Question 5. First, you want to know who the other trusted advisors are in the client's life. From a competitive perspective and a client-influence perspective, you have to identify and understand who else has your client's ear and business so you know where you stand relative to them.

Second, when we study the best in the business—those who are most successful—what we notice is that they have a network of professionals with whom they partner so that they can provide comprehensive wealth management. The answer to Question 5 will provide you with essential data for building your network of professionals with whom you partner.

Note that I am not talking about the old, trite centers of influence or professional alliances for the benefit of getting referrals. Referrals are not even what you want. What you really want are introductions, and you only get formal introductions if you have professional partnerships with people.

By asking Question 5 of your clients, you will be able to gather key information that will help you in the reframe to develop those professional partnerships and to provide complete wealth management. The reality is that if you are going to deliver wealth management, you will likely specialize in only one piece of wealth management and need to build out a team for the rest.

For example, if you are a financial planner, you may still need on your team a primary banker, a primary insurance agent, a primary business valuation specialist, a health care consultant, a person to handle the concentrated stock position, and more. As your client goes through one or more life transitions, you are likely to have a need to connect him or her to one of these other professionals on your team. If you are proactive about building this team, all roads can lead back to you as the financial planner or wealth advisor.

The best way to build this network is to ask your existing clients, "Hey, by the way, among your other trusted advisors, who do you trust the most and why? Because from time to time, my clients need to connect with these other types of professionals, and the way we have built our network is by asking our clients who they trust the most and why, to determine whether or not we want to add them to our professional network for the benefit of our clients, because we are building a community—a community of clients and a community of profession-als that together can help our clients achieve their goals and dreams and hopes and desires."

As you are building your network, you are also creating goodwill with the clients and deepening their potential to trust in you—to un-derstand that you will truly be able to take care of them because you have a robust team, not just of partners, but of partners that your clients trust.

KEY CONCEPT

Finding out which other professionals are advising your clients lets you know where you stand with your clients and provides the potential opportunity to expand your professional network.

COACHING CORNER

Imagine that during the ClientWise Conversation™, a client tells you several areas where he has been disappointed with your firm, and in the process he expresses that he has even considered leaving your firm. How would you respond to such a client during the conversation? Let this scenario play out in your mind, or even better, role-play it with a colleague so you can practice responding out loud.

The Meeting Wrap-Up

As the meeting comes to a close, you will want to let the client know that his or her input was really valuable and helpful. Do not forget to thank your client for his or her time, ideas, and candor. Plan, too, to ask permission of the client to be able to have a follow-up conversa-tion in the future with a question like one of the following. (That be-ing said, there are some clients you will not go back to because they weren't really helpful. If you feel this is the case for a particular client, you can skip this step.)

"Would it be okay if we circle back to you in a couple of months and share with you our key findings?"

"Would it be okay if we came back to you and demonstrated some of the items we are improving, perhaps [from a technology perspective or from a processing perspective or from a messaging perspective]?"

"Would it be all right if I come back and share with you regarding the value that we really want to bring to our clients?"

"Would you mind my sharing those key insights and what changes and improvements we have decided to make?"

"I have some work to do. Thanks for your input. I want to come back to you after I've done some thinking and learning because we want to reshape, we're improving, and we want to include you in the improving part of the process so you're aware of what we've done; is that OK?"

By closing in this way, you will demonstrate that you are taking the client and his or her opinion seriously and that this is not simply a matter of you looking to get referrals from the client. It conveys that you are engaging in an authentically driven process around identifying how you are being framed today.

In addition to going back to your client in the future with the results of your reframe, plan to make it a habit as a team, every 18 to 20 months, to have this kind of conversation with your client. This will allow you to get a fresh read on how you are being framed at that stage in time and to identify whether steps you've taken to reframe your business are working.

 From ClientWise Conversation™ to Analysis

You made the calls, you scheduled the visits, you kept the appointments, you had the conversations. You've got a pile of notes and ringing ears, and the question that arises is, "Now what?" Gathering data was only step 1; now you need to make sense of it all. That is, you need to analyze your data.

Start by reviewing what you wrote. Think back to what your clients said and how they said it. With everything refreshed in your mind, begin to do the following:

- Look for patterns in client responses.
- Ask the team for input on the client responses.
- Ask yourself, what words and phrases did you hear?
- Identify the gaps between how the client frames you and how you want to be framed.
- Determine how you and the team can use what you have discovered in your daily work, beginning right now.
- Start documenting what you achieve each and every quarter with the client.

Mentally processing all of the information and using it to make changes to your practice (during future steps of the reframing process) will not be an overnight operation, so be patient with yourself. In some cases, at some point in the future, circumstances may trigger a memory of a client comment, and you may have an "aha!" moment when the significance or application of the client's observation suddenly makes sense. Think of this analyzing process as a marathon, not a sprint. Use what you can, when you can, and accept that if something does not make sense now, it may in the future.

CONCLUSION

In reality, your clients may not understand exactly what it is that you do. They may not realize the unique nature of your value proposition, or they may find it difficult to articulate what it is you do that is different from the thousands of other financial advisors in the marketplace. The only way to find out whether this is the case is by taking the time to talk with them. That's what step 1 of the reframing process is all about.

It's a powerful opportunity to be in conversation with your best clients in a new and different way. There's no discussion of investments, financial planning, or the capital markets; you are meeting with the clients to invite them to provide you feedback about you and your practice.

In the process, you will gather data that allows you to create a baseline of how you are being framed. You will have a rich pool of information that you can analyze and identify patterns in how your clients view your services, what they value most about you, and the things they would like to see you change. In step 2, you will spend time defining what you would like your new frame to be. With the baseline for how others are framing you at the ready and your new vision for how you want to be framed, you'll be set to close the gap. No longer will you have to guess at how to frame yourself for clients; you'll have the information needed to create your desired reframe.

NOTES

1. Tom Weilert, personal interview, March 13, 2015, transcript, pp. 10–11.
2. Janice Wood, "Compliments Can Improve Performance," *PsychCentral*, November 11, 2011, accessed March 25, 2015, http://psychcentral.com/news/2012/11/11/compliments-can-improve-performance/47462.html.
3. As quoted in Alina Tugend, "Too Many Choices: A Problem That Can Paralyze," *New York Times*, February 26, 2010, www.nytimes.com/2010/02/27/your-money/27shortcuts.html?_r=1.
4. Jonathan Beukelman, personal interview, March 13, 2015, transcript, p. 3.
5. Ibid., p. 4.
6. Ibid.

CHAPTER 7

Defining Your New Frame by Discovering Your Value

I f you've completed step 1 of the reframing process, you've done the meaningful work of collecting and analyzing a large amount of information from your clients and the professionals with whom you work and interact. You've looked for significant patterns and taken note of important gaps. You know what it is that clients value about your services, and you know the areas where they would seek you to make changes. In all, you now have a tremendous pool of information that you can use to inform you as you *define your new frame*. That's step 2 of the reframing process (see Figure 7.1).

The information in step 1 of the reframing process has come from the outside, so to speak—from your clients and the other professionals you have interviewed. Now it's time to look within yourself, your team, and the organization for wisdom and guidance on what you believe a good reframe will be for the firm. The data you have gathered from

Figure 7.1 Reframe Step 2: Define Your New Frame

clients and professionals, coupled with the insights and ideas you generate by brainstorming internally with your team, will provide you with the valuable information you need to define an effective frame that supports your clients in a way that works for them and, at the same time, is reflective of a purpose you and your team are excited to fulfill.

How will you ultimately decide to define your new frame? Maybe you have a passion for helping entrepreneurs and decide to reframe yourself as an advisory firm dedicated to serving small to midsize organizations with an entrepreneurial bent by offering cash management, liability management, asset transfer, and other services this group needs. Maybe you will choose to reframe as a firm that provides support to professional athletes on signing bonuses, budgeting, retirement planning, and more. You might instead choose to cater to family-owned businesses or to ultra-high-net-worth millennials, providing services customized just for them. The frame you define will be as unique as you and your team, your strengths, your interests, and your clients.

Erin Botsford, CEO and founder of Botsford Financial Group, has framed her firm on the basis of some of her significant experiences growing up. When Botsford was 11 years old, her father died and left her mother with six kids and a $10,000 life insurance policy.[1] Botsford and her family went from middle-class status to poverty in an instant. When Botsford was 16 years old, she was in a car accident in which she collided with a man on a motorcycle; the motorcyclist died in the crash. Her mother had to put a second mortgage on their home to pay for the fees to defend Botsford, who was eventually found innocent.

On the basis of these and other early life experiences, Botsford developed an outlook that risk management was the core of the financial advisory work she did with clients. In her words, her firm's "entire focus is helping people protect their money, their assets, and their life's work."[2] Not surprisingly, the tagline after her company name on her website reads, "the keepers and protectors of our clients' lifestyles, as they define them.™" Last, the company bio explains, "The Botsford Group is a comprehensive wealth management firm, specializing in Asset Protection and Risk Management strategies for business owners and senior executives of Fortune 500 companies."[3] How's that for a clear frame, designed to take the best care of Botsford's clients, in a way that Botsford can authentically stand behind?

Like Botsford, you can specialize in working with your ideal clients in a way that is supportive to them while also being grounded in the authentic purpose of your team. You get there by defining and building the right frame. Having interviewed your clients in step 1 of the reframe using the ClientWise Conversation™, you're off to a great start. This chapter will provide you with six questions you can use to interview yourself and your own team to define your new frame in a customized way that works for both you and your clients.

The ultimate goal of defining the right frame for your firm and your clients is to be able to provide true value to your clients. By taking the time to define your new frame (and, later, to build it), you will be able to regularly generate value that is unique to your firm and that provides your ideal clients with just what they need to be successful.

Note, too, that this process of defining a new frame for your firm is durable and can be used again and again. The best in the business are always looking for ways to adjust and improve, and one of the effective ways to do that is to tweak and redefine one's frame. Therefore, think of the frame-defining step not as a one-time event but rather as a process that can be used over and over again to refine and improve the

KEY CONCEPT

Before you can build a new frame, you need to figure out what you have to offer and what the clients you want to serve need. This information will come from internal and external sources. Look at the information you have already gathered with an open mind, let it guide you and your thinking as you prepare to reframe, and remember that your goal in the reframe is to provide true value to your clients.

frame. If you're committed to building enterprise value, teach those at your firm to consistently listen, grow, and improve. Now, that's sustainable!

You know how your clients frame your firm because you've interviewed them with the ClientWise Conversation™. With that valuable information at the forefront of your mind, you are ready to look inward and ask yourself and your team the following six questions to continue the exploration process and determine how best to define your new frame (see Figure 7.2).

First, *what is your noble purpose?* What are you trying to meaningfully accomplish by running your organization, beyond making a good living for yourself and your team? Why does your firm exist? Knowing your noble purpose will give you a foundation you can return to time and again as you ask yourself the remainder of the questions needed to define your new frame.

Second, *who do you want your business to be built to serve?* Who are you passionate about supporting? Another way of asking this question is, who is your ideal client? You can determine your ideal client by identifying your specific target group, your niche within that target group, and then your ideal clients within that niche. Once you know who your firm is going to be built to serve, you are ever closer to defining your new frame.

Once you've identified the group you would like to build your business to serve, ask *what are this group's main concern(s)?* With this question, the goal is to identify the needs of your ideal client types.

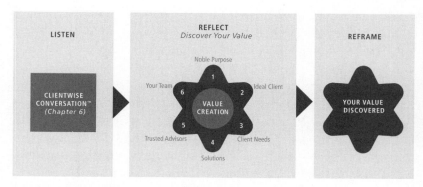

Figure 7.2 The Wealth Management Reframe Process

Here's another way to ask the question: What do you know that your ideal clients need that they don't even know they need, because you're an expert in working with them? You can start with your ideal clients' main concern/s and, from there, break that down into their various needs—both known and unknown.

With this valuable information in hand, you will be ready to ask yourself, *What solutions or solutions will you provide to your ideal clients?* It's brainstorming time. Recognize a client need? Find a solution. But, first, let's be clear here. Solutions are not just the *products* that you are compensated for delivering, they're also the *services* you are or are not compensated for delivering. What custom services do you provide? What intellectual capital do you offer? Value occurs not only in the products you offer but also in the services you provide through your firm's signature approach.

Next, to deliver the desired solutions to your ideal clients with your signature approach, it's likely you will want and need to invite other trusted advisors into the process. Unless you are ready to grow into a mega-organization, chances are you will want or need to build out a strong professional network to be able to truly serve your clients' full spectrum of needs. That's where the next question comes in as you are defining your new frame: *What other trusted advisors work with your ideal clients?* Part of your value to the client is to serve as a facilitator: The root of this word is *facile,* which means "easy." How much easier can you make your clients' lives by identifying the other advisors with whom they need to work and by developing a relationship with these advisors so that you can make them even more available to your clients and at just the right times?

Asking Questions 2, 3, 4, and 5 as you define your new frame can generate some fascinating and useful results. A number of years ago, I conducted a series of workshops with several groups of more than 50 advisors each over the course of several months in Princeton, New Jersey, that used this process to help them define their new frames. The room was abuzz with conversation, creativity, and innovation. All in all, the groups generated more than 25 pages of ideas, focused on more than 35 different target client groups. Take a look at some of the unique results that these advisors generated toward possible future reframes (see Table 7.1).

Table 7.1 Sample Work of Advisors Brainstorming About the Needs and Solutions of Their Ideal Clients and About Their Trusted Advisors

Target Market	Needs	Solutions	Trusted Advisors
Real estate developers	Known: ■ Estate planning ■ Diversification ■ Confidentiality ■ Multiple existing advisor relationships ■ Sophistication ■ Tax sensitivity Unknown: ■ Leverage ■ Life insurance ■ Tax strategies ■ Consolidation of financial picture	Known: ■ International trust ■ Offshore products ■ Wealth management tools ■ Multicurrency ■ Airplane financing ■ Mortgage of multiple residences Unknown (intangible): ■ Referral to international corporate finance group ■ Doing business in native language ■ Expertise in doing cross-border transactions ■ Personal representations	■ Real estate agent ■ Materials/construction owners ■ Government agencies ■ Existing clients in sector ■ Bankers ■ Chamber of Commerce ■ Professional associations
Lawyers	Known: ■ High taxable income ■ Time management ■ Irregular cash flow ■ Disability insurance ■ Stock options/stock concentration Unknown: ■ 401(k) (but no pension stream) ■ Board of directors exposure ■ Estate planning, tax treatment of life insurance	■ High taxable income review, fixed income strategy, max retirement contribution ■ Irregular cash flow & estimated tax issue—managed cash reserve ■ Stock concentration—prepaid forward, exchange funds, charitable swing ■ 401(k)/pension-structure retirement income ■ Board of directors exposure, Sarbanes–Oxley ■ Estate planning & life insurance, ILIT	■ Real estate broker ■ Insurance broker ■ Employment lawyer

Target Market	Needs	Solutions	Trusted Advisors
People with philanthropic interests	Known: ■ Current and planned giving ■ Make a difference ■ Leave a legacy ■ Tax sensitivity Unknown: ■ How charitable gifts affect their overall financial and estate plan ■ How to maximize your charitable gifts	■ Proactive approach to maximize charitable giving ■ Ongoing relationships, not transactional ■ Identify center for philanthropy ■ Specific vehicles	■ Estate attorney ■ CPA ■ Professional fundraiser ■ Directors of planned giving ■ Family foundations

Table 7.1 captures sample answers to the Questions 2–5 in the frame-defining process:

1. What is your noble purpose?
2. Who do you want your business to be built to serve (ideal clients)?
3. What are this group's main concern/s (and related needs)?
4. What solution or solutions will you provide to your ideal clients?
5. What other trusted advisors work with your ideal clients?

Once advisors and firms have gotten clear on their noble purpose, ideal clients, needs, solutions, and professional networks, advisors can ask the last question of the frame-defining process:

6. What team would you like to build to fulfill your noble purpose?

With Question 6, you will identify what kind of a team you will need to build to fulfill your noble purpose and deliver the promised value to your ideal client. Once all six of these questions are answered, you will be well positioned to authentically describe who you serve and what you stand for, which conveys the new frame in a nutshell and will be used to inform all of the marketing material that gets built during the next part of the reframing process.

THE eXchange™

Online Tool 7.1: Example Needs, Target Market, Solutions, and Centers of Influence

There's no replacement for what can be created by great minds working together in a single room. The information generated in Table 7.1 on the different target groups advisors can work with, along with their associated needs, solutions, and centers of influence, is evidence of that. Download this amazing free content from the eXchange™ (youvebeenframed.clientwise.com) to help get your own creative juices flowing as you define your new frame.

KEY CONCEPT

Once you have defined your noble purpose, identified your ideal clients, understood their needs, brainstormed solutions to their problems, built a strong professional network to support you and your clients, created a team to deliver your value, and can authentically describe what you do and who you do it for, what you need to do to reframe will be clear.

QUESTION 1: WHAT IS YOUR NOBLE PURPOSE?

By now, you know that my view is that the work that financial advisors do, when done well, is truly noble work. I say this because I've been a witness to greatness by many financial professionals who have genuinely helped clients build and implement successful financial plans that have helped those clients get a clear vision about what they wanted to achieve and take those necessary steps to attain the results they had hoped for. When an advisory team does their work well, they impact hundreds, perhaps even thousands, of families: They can change communities. In fact, when they do their work really well, they create sustainable firms using effective succession planning and employ those next-generation advisors who can connect to the heirs of their clients' wealth and impact generations to come.

When defining your new frame, start with the purpose of your firm. It's the purpose that keeps the team focused on the prize, serving others. It's the purpose that keeps the other trusted advisors with whom the advisory team has chosen to partner for the benefit of the clients trustful of that professional partnership for the benefit of others. It's the purpose that allows for successful client acquisition strategies to work with ease.

The purpose should be an ambition that is significant in size, aspirational in scope, and possible to achieve that will serve your clients, yourself, and your organization. For example, a firm's purpose might be to help as many individuals as possible, including ourselves, to develop sufficient financial freedom to be able to engage in work or play driven only by their passion, rather than settled for because of need, by the time they are sixty years old. You get the picture. Significant in size. Aspirational in scope. Possible to achieve.

There is a sense of nobility in the purposeful work of financial advisors that I often observe but isn't well articulated by the advisor or advisory team. Yet it's my view that the team's purpose ought to be central to the frame. As we coach in our Lone Ranger to Leader™ programs at ClientWise, the common purpose and intent make up the larger, more inspiring ideas and aims that will drive your team's definition of wealth management, who the ideal client is, what products and services your team chooses to offer, the intellectual property and signature approach that your team will design and implement, and what the team's client service model is. The purpose is what will guide how you build the team that will serve your clients as well.

 ## COACHING CORNER

What is your firm's noble purpose? Take time on your own with pen and paper to reflect on this question and to sketch it out; bring your team together to explore this question and discuss. The next chapter of this book also provides details on how to work with your team to identify a common purpose. Begin this process now, as it will provide you with the foundation for defining the rest of your frame.

KEY CONCEPT

Your firm's noble purpose can be the central, inspirational point around which you and your team revolve. That purpose should be significant in size, aspirational in scope, and possible to achieve to the benefit of your clients, yourself, and your organization.

QUESTION 2: WHO'S YOUR IDEAL CLIENT?

Now that you know what your noble purpose is, you are ready to answer the question, whom do you want your firm built to serve? In simpler terms, who, exactly, is your client? There's a very good reason why redefining begins with getting clear on who your target client is—because your job as a firm is to provide value to your clients, and the only way to do that is to understand whom you are working with. Only when you understand this can you determine their needs and thus know what solutions to provide. The value is in the solutions!

Having a specific client you are serving will affect your entire approach to your business. So, it's time to brainstorm on your target market and, from there, create your ideal client profile. Within a target market, there are niches, and within those niches, there are ideal clients. For example, say you have identified dentists as the target market. Yet within the category of dentists are a variety of specialists, such as general dentists, oral pathologists, periodontists, orthodontists, endodontists, pedodontists, oral and maxillofacial surgeons, and so on. Within those niches, there is an ideal client type for your firm; this is the kind of person you'd like to work with in terms of their characteristics, attitude, outlook, demographics, and more. For example, you may choose to serve periodontists who (ideal client type) live in the Northeast, have families, want to retire by 50 years of age, and enjoy investing their money but want a partner to ensure they make smart decisions.

Plan to do this ideal client brainstorming activity with your team—led by you, someone on your team, or even a coaching or consulting firm. Start by taking a look at the top 50 clients of your firm. Look for patterns of how you met them, what you like about them, what you may dislike about them, how much energy and time they require, who excites you, who you enjoy speaking with, and who your team despises when their name comes up on the caller ID. There will be groups of individuals that you enjoy serving most, and then there will be those that you may find difficult to serve. This is a very good exercise for a person to consider when identifying the ideal client type.

Some things you may want to consider when going through this client analysis are the following:

- Do you enjoy haggling over fees?
- When you explain your fee structure, which clients ask tough questions but value your services?
- Who understands the rising expenses associated with running a financial advisory firm?
- Who couldn't care less and doesn't want you to meet with their children, grandchildren, or heirs?
- Who finds it easy to introduce you to their friends and colleagues?
- Who wants no part in thinking about helping your firm grow and doesn't understand the benefits when your firm does grow?
- If you could work with any individual client, who would it be and why?
- Think of one of your favorite clients and write down a list of characteristics that make this client unique. Repeat as desired.
- What are the characteristics and demographics of your ideal client (e.g., age, gender, career field, education level, geographic location)?

The results of engaging in this exercise may surprise you or they may seem excitingly right on track. Either way, they will provide you with a clear starting point for identifying your ideal clients and defining your new frame.

KEY CONCEPT

Identify your target niche market as well as the characteristics that define your ideal client. The diamonds will be found in the details.

Here's a look at some of the unique and varied target market niches that were generated by the same group of advisors who created the materials shown in Table 7.1: Asian business owners, special needs associations, aircraft owners, women in transition (widows, divorcees, new-job hunters), trucking company owners, oil executives, farmers/ranchers/landowners, NFL and PGA athletes, lobbyists, and tribal governments. As you can see, no target client was off limits when these advisors gave themselves time and space to brainstorm about the possibilities. Table 7.2 shows additional example target markets and niches, along with example ideal client types.

I'm often asked, can my firm serve only one type of ideal client? The answer is, of course. It's your firm. You get to choose. But in doing so, consider how you will scale and build a firm that is profitable, sustainable, and long lasting while serving a single type of ideal client. Think about what types of services and service models will allow you to render something more complex and of high value to your ideal client. Alternatively, you may find that team members can play a number of technical roles that serve a variety of ideal client types. For example, managing investment portfolios is a professional service that can be centralized, while the advisors in the firm can deliver customized services for each ideal client type, such as the financial planning and relationship management.

Table 7.2 Examples of Target Markets, Niches, and Ideal Client Types

Target Market	Niche	Ideal Client
C-suite execs	IT industry	West Coast based, workaholic seeking more work–life balance, within five years of retirement
Women	Working mothers who are 40+ years old	Full-time employed, worried about saving for college, appreciates the value of advice
Professional athletes	Football players	Been injured, so appreciates the finite aspect of their career; humble; good sense of humor; effective communicator
Nonprofit leaders	Leads a health-related agency	U.S. based with international travel, master's degree or above, excellent business sense

Who will your ideal client be? By setting aside time on your and the team's calendars to ask and answer this question, you will gain essential information needed to define your new frame.

COACHING CORNER

What group of individuals would you like to serve as your clients and why? Start with your ideal target market and, from there, narrow down to your ideal target niche or niches. Next, think about your ideal clients' age, interests, demographics, characteristics, and any other descriptors that make them unique and of interest to you as clients. As you work through this exercise, feel free to write down as many answers as come to mind. Later, review them and circle those that most excite you, then rank order them. Which ideal clients are you starting to focus on?

QUESTION 3: WHAT ARE YOUR CLIENTS' NEEDS?

Once you have determined who your ideal client is, you are ready to move on to exploring with your team what your clients' needs are. This step is essential. If you don't know what your clients' needs are, then you may well end up providing services and solutions that are of no use or interest to them.

It's like standing on a street corner in northern Alaska selling beach equipment straight from a Florida beachside stand. You may be very proud of offering the best suntan lotion, sunglasses, towels, beach chairs, and beach umbrellas, but your clients, who don't value these things, will be scratching their heads and saying to you, "But we don't do the beach here." Your clients, in this situation, need parkas and winter hats with flappy ears, not picnic coolers and popsicles. It's a case of misaligned services and client needs and no one—neither the advisor nor the client—wants that. While this is an extreme example, you get the point.

Looking at Figure 7.3, you can see how offering the wrong kind of services to your particular clients will lead to a miss in terms of client satisfaction. You can provide the most excellent version of your services, but if the client doesn't need them, who cares? Certainly not the client.

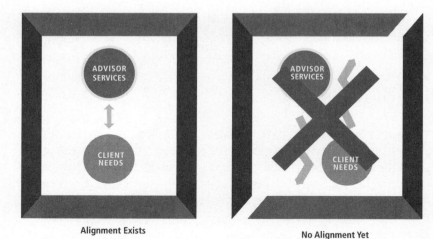

Figure 7.3 Aligned versus Unaligned Advisor Services and Client Needs

The reality is that if you provide services that your clients don't need or value, you will struggle to retain clients or gain new ones. On the flip side, if you provide services that your clients want, need, and value, they will be willing to pay you today and tomorrow. That's a win–win situation for everyone.

Here are some questions you can ask yourself and the team to identify your clients needs:

- What kind of support does your client need to successfully manage his or her wealth?
- What would make your client sleep better at night or jump for joy in the morning when it comes to finance-related matters?
- What services can you provide to ensure your client avoids future pitfalls and challenges? Any others that you can think of to add?
- What needs does your client have without even realizing it?

Identifying your clients' needs sets you up to provide solutions to them. Who doesn't want to have their needs met? Solutions and support equal satisfied clients who remain loyal to the organization.

KEY CONCEPT

After you've identified your ideal target clients, put in the work to figure out the specific client needs within your chosen niche. Taking the time to understand your client is the first step in serving that client.

Here are some example client needs (see Table 7.3) generated by the group of advisors who brainstormed the data revealed in Table 7.1.

Table 7.3 Examples of Client Needs

Target Market	Needs
Business owners	Known: ■ Taxes ■ Profitability ■ Liquidity ■ Cash management ■ Retirement benefits ■ Making payroll Unknown: ■ Costs of cash management ■ Succession plan ■ Exit strategy ■ Liquidity strategy—family ■ Estate planning/asset protection ■ Organizing personal life ■ Holistic vs. atomistic ■ Lending capabilities
Asian business owners	Known: ■ Retirement planning ■ Estate tax issue ■ Currency ■ Risk of political issues ■ Language barrier Unknown: ■ Liability ■ Insurance ■ Estate presentation ■ Currency hedge ■ Offshore strategy

(Continued)

Table 7.3 (*Continued*)

Target Market	Needs
Aircraft owners	Known: ▪ Financing needs ▪ Refurbishing ▪ System upgrades Unknown: ▪ Upgrade ▪ Types of financing
Blue-collar retirees with large 401(k)s	Known: ▪ Structuring income ▪ Estate planning ▪ Largest source of liquid assets Unknown: ▪ Multiple cash flow solutions ▪ Minimize adverse tax consequences

As you explore your clients' needs, don't stop at the surface or the obvious. Dig deeper, investigating the unknown needs of your clients, too. That is where the magic is. The clients don't know what they don't know, but if you're an expert at serving those clients, you likely have insights into the things your clients need that they don't even know they need.

These unknown needs are where an advisor can provide real value. Let's go back to our dentist example. Perhaps your firm is built to serve small- to medium-sized dentistry practices. The dentists at a particular practice have done a good job setting up a retirement plan for themselves and their staff. But what they don't know is the importance of insurance-related services, or what their succession strategy is, or what continuity planning is about, or what their exit strategy is, or how to value the business, or how to set up an ownership structure that would allow the sale of the business internally or externally with ease.

But with your research, experience, and expertise, your firm has built a network of business valuation specialists, attorneys, and insurance professionals who specialize, like you, in serving this target market. Because of your approach, you've worked out an arrangement with this group of professionals. All of you have agreed who your ideal client really is, and together you believe you can serve this group more effectively than any other wealth management group out there. You see, the unknown needs are where the value is.

Supporting your clients' unknown needs is a huge part of the value you will be providing once you deliver on your new frame! You can set yourself up for success in the future by uncovering your clients' known and unknown needs now.

Last, don't forget about all that valuable data you gathered during the ClientWise Conversation™. Take a look back at the results from those conversations and pull out the varying needs that your clients evidenced there. There is no more reliable data on your clients than that they've given you themselves. So where the needs are relevant to your ideal client profile, plan to pull those into your new frame.

 ## INDUSTRY INSIGHT: DEFINING YOUR BRAND ON THE BASIS OF YOUR BELIEFS

When asked for his thoughts on how advisors can go about successfully framing themselves, Gregory Mech, managing director at The CAPROCK Group, naturally drifted to the notion that the process has to begin with one's values. Mech explained, "It becomes really important as we enter an exercise like reframing that we understand our own values, our own beliefs, and . . . what our higher purpose is because that's going to be the foundation from which all of our behaviors radiate."[4] In contrast, Mech believes that many times the process of rebranding or reframing "becomes an exercise in advertising or spin."[5] Such an approach is, in his view, misplaced.

For Mech, it's about authenticity. "The thing that comes to mind for me, as I think about rebranding and reframing," Mech described, "is just because you say you are doesn't mean you are."[6] He referenced the example of Tesla Motors versus Fisker Automotive: two automobile companies that each promised the public that they would provide a luxury automobile that was environmentally sound. Tesla followed through and sold more than 2,250 Roadsters in 31 countries between 2008 and March 2012;[7] Fisker crashed and burned after a two-year delay, a release in 2011, and then a production stop in 2012 due to a lack of financial resources.[8]

Mech believes that many financial services firms fall into the same trap as Fisker: framing themselves a certain way without then delivering on that frame. In Mech's view, it's a recipe for disaster. He has taken a different approach and it has worked for him.

(Continued)

(*Continued*)

Mech frames his work today in a way that meshes with his values and beliefs—and then he delivers. He noted, "I help families discover and understand what matters most to them, and then I help them fulfill whatever that goal or destiny might be. That fits with me because I . . . believe I'm here to help steward clients who don't necessarily have the financial intelligence to get to where they want to go, to help them make good decisions, to act as their advocate." According to Mech, his clients will confirm that he does just that. As he explained, "That's an important distinction . . . because unless people have that mutual understanding or agreement that, in fact, that is your brand and that is what is delivered by the brand . . . it's not meaningful."[9]

QUESTION 4: WHAT SOLUTIONS DO YOU PROVIDE?

With your clients' needs identified, you are ready to move on to what *solutions* you are going to provide your clients. These are the things your clients are going to pay you for. Now it's all about your creating value for your client.

No longer are you subjected to a guessing game on what kind of solutions to provide for your clients, because the work you've done in defining their needs has set you up for success. All you need to do is take the time with your team to consider the solutions to which these needs logically point.

 KEY CONCEPT

Knowing the needs of your client means you're halfway to serving that client. Commit to finding and providing the solutions to their problems.

Let's say your ideal clients are women in transition (women who have been widowed, have divorced, lost a job, are changing jobs, and others) and one of their *needs* is to manage their money so it lasts. The question becomes, what kind of *solutions* can you provide to help these clients ensure that their money indeed lasts over the long haul? This question could be answered a number of ways, depending on the firm, its strengths, and its vision. Here is what the test group of 50 advisors came up with:

- Spending plan
- Retirement income service
- Women's education
- Quarterly seminars
- Long-term care
- Annuities
- Portfolio management
- Estate plan
- Trusted IRA
- Tax issue guidance
- Social connection/emotional empathy

What services would you come up with? However you answer this question will help you further clarify what your frame has the potential to look like in the future.

Another way to look at this piece of the framing process is as defining what wealth management looks like for your firm. You know that wealth management is more than investment management or sales; you know that true wealth management is meant to be comprehensive. What needs to be clarified now is how you want to define wealth management for your firm. Here are some questions to help you and your team engage in this part of the process:

- Look at each of the needs of your clients. What one or more solutions do you believe could address each need?
- If the client were your son, daughter, niece, nephew, dear friend, or anyone that you cared about deeply, what kind of solutions would you want to make sure they had access to?
- Imagine you had unlimited time, human capital, and money at your disposal. What kind of solutions would you be excited about developing, providing, and/or connecting your client to?
- Imagine you are at a conference dedicated to your ideal client type, and you display a poster with all of the solutions you can provide for this group. List 10 items that you'd be sure to put on this list.

As you work through this piece of the process, give yourself the freedom to imagine anything and everything. Brainstorm in a team setting and/or in solitude with a blank sheet of paper and a pen, with a plan to take it into the team setting at a later time. Think about how you brainstorm best and get others on your team involved, too. Bottom line: The sky's the limit during this idea stage, so plan to set all constraints, concerns, and reality checks aside.

 What to Do When Your Current Clients Don't Need Your Services

At the core of defining a new frame for your team and your firm is the process of aligning the kind of services your clients need and the kind of services you are willing, interested, and able to provide. As you engage in the process of defining your new frame, it will become clear to you whether the services you currently provide match up with your ideal client profile. If not, that's a sign that something's gotta give. There are only two ways out of the dilemma: Change your clients or change your services! The answer is up to you, but if a gap is discovered, this issue must be addressed.

While considering what solutions you will be providing to your ideal clients, think, too, about the development of your own intellectual property. For example, you may have developed a specific approach to wealth management that you've named and that you can trademark if you haven't already. You may have a step-by-step planning process, designed to help a business owner exit his or her business, that you can document and formalize. Or you may have knowledge that you can convert into checklists, questionnaires, and assessments that you can give to your clients to help them make decisions about how best to manage their wealth.

 INDUSTRY INSIGHT: TURNING INTELLECTUAL CAPITAL INTO INTELLECTUAL PROPERTY

Michael Tannery, cofounder and CEO of Tannery & Company Wealth Management, has done a fantastic job of turning his company's ideas and processes into intellectual property that his firm can use to win new business and also share with existing clients so they can better manage their wealth.

One of the novel ideas that turned into a product Tannery and his firm created is a workbook titled *I Was Married, I Got a Divorce, I'm a Success.* The father of three children, Tannery went through his own divorce 17 years ago, during which he experienced the emotional and financial issues associated with being a divorced parent. Tannery used this experience to create a workbook that his firm now gives to its clients who are undergoing a divorce.

The book has 12 exercises focused on not just the financial aspects of divorce but the emotional aspects, too. Tannery explained that after his divorce, "what I understood wasn't just the financial side . . . I understood the emotional timeline that occurs."[10] Tannery took that knowledge and created a book that helps his clients.

This workbook also helps Tannery open the door to lasting partnerships with other professionals. When he and his team call on family lawyers, they give them this book. The lawyers quickly realize that this is a differentiating factor for Tannery's firm versus other financial services firms they typically encounter.

Tannery is also sure to share success stories of the way he has been able to help his divorcing clients. One of his favorites is how he was able to help two clients swap houses: a client in the middle of a divorce who needed to downsize and another client who was ready to upsize. In the process, Tannery saved both clients a total of $60,000 in real estate commissions.

Another favorite success story is the time one of his clients, a divorced woman, asked for suggestions on how to collect an outstanding business bill from a client. After taking Tannery's advice and successfully obtaining the check (in the thousands of dollars), the woman called Tannery to thank him and said before hanging up, "You are the best husband I never had. I love you."[11] She called right back, at which point Tannery said, "It's okay, I love you too," and they laughed. Tannery describes this kind of relationship with the client as not being "a romantic love, but it's just an incredible connection and trust because they know that we're here for them no matter what's going on." Tannery gets that the value of his firm to his clients is first and foremost the trusting relationship.

In sharing these client-centered success stories, along with his divorce workbook, with the professionals he is courting to become part of his network, Tannery frames his firm as a true advocate for the client. Not surprisingly, he finds that these professionals are interested in learning more about partnering with him.

COACHING CORNER

Pick your favorite questions in the previous two sections on identifying client needs and generating solutions. Grab a blank sheet of paper or open up your computer and write the answers. Alternatively, find a colleague to do this exercise with and talk through it out loud.

QUESTION 5: WHAT OTHER TRUSTED ADVISORS WORK WITH YOUR TARGET GROUP?

After all of that productive brainstorming, you may have a substantial list of possible solutions you can provide to your target client. Before fears can possibly take over and stop you in your tracks with questions like, "How am I going to deliver all of these services?" or "Is my team really up to the challenge?" you can work on answering with your team the next question involved in defining your new frame: Which other trusted advisors work with your target group?

These trusted advisors are an important piece of your new frame. Once you get them on board, you can turn that wish list of client solutions into true wealth management that you, your firm, and your professional network can deliver. Check out the following list of trusted professionals that my test group of 50 advisors generated for their target clients of women executives.

CPAs	Recruiters/ headhunters	Contractors
Attorneys		Architects
Divorce attorneys	Insurance specialists	Salon/day spa employees
Psychologists	Human resources	
Physicians	Bankers	Teachers, camp counselors
Spiritual counselors	IT specialists	
Advertising/PR firms	Commercial realtors	American Business Women's Association
Women's organizations	Interior designers	

National Association of Women Business Owners	Affinity groups within corporations	Churches
Chamber of Commerce	Business journals and industries	Book clubs
	Women's magazines and periodicals	Meetup.com
		Volunteer/ community services
		Alumnae

How's that for being thorough? Your list does not need to be as long as this one, but it does show how expansive one's thinking can be when engaging in this exercise.

There is nothing fancy or complex about generating a list of trusted professionals for your target market. It's a matter of taking the time to think this piece through. Here are a few questions to help you and your team work through this step with ease.

- Look at each solution you've written down for your target clients. What kind of professional/s would be in a good position to offer that solution?

- Think about the other professionals you currently have a relationship with or have always meant to reach out to. Which of these professionals would be well suited to offer additional support to your target client?

- Pull out the data collected as you were engaging in the Client-Wise Conversation™. What trusted advisors did your clients share then who also would be suited to supporting your newly identified target client?

Because their wealth management needs are diverse, clients most likely need support from more than you and your firm, yet they probably don't want to have to look elsewhere. If you can take the guesswork out of whom else they should be talking to and introduce them to other trusted professionals who can support them, your clients' trust and appreciation of you will grow. And in the future, when they need another service or introduction, who will they naturally go to? You. That puts you in a position to provide them with additional services, make other introductions, build more goodwill, and allow the cycle of loyalty to continue.

KEY CONCEPT

It may be impossible for your firm to provide every single service that your clients need. Building a network of professionals to whom you can refer clients for the services you don't cover still leaves you in the position of being the answer to your clients' questions. This is a good position from which to build trust, goodwill, rapport, satisfaction, and loyalty.

QUESTION 6: WHAT TEAM WOULD YOU LIKE TO BUILD TO FULFILL YOUR NOBLE PURPOSE?

You know what your noble purpose is, who your ideal client is, what their known and unknown needs are, what solutions you'd like to provide them to meet their needs, and who the trusted advisors are that can help in effectively providing these solutions to your clients. You are ready to determine what team you will need and want to build to fulfill your noble purpose and support the needs of your ideal clients. The following chapter will guide you on how to fully address Question 6. But for now, start to think about what kind of team you will need to form. You've already started to consider what trusted advisors to add to your network or external team, so begin to think about who will need to be on your internal team. What kind of professionals will you want to hire; what roles will need to be filled; and what traits, values, and characteristics do you want to add to your team?

KEY CONCEPT

The previous steps of redefining your frame have identified your noble purpose, who your ideal client is, what your clients need, what you can provide, and what other services your professional network enables. The final step of defining your new frame is to figure out who you need on your firm's internal team to meet the needs of your clients.

CAPTURING YOUR VALUE

When it comes to defining your new frame, the sum of the whole is greater than any individual part. When you bring together your noble purpose, your ideal client, the solutions you provide to meet the needs of your ideal clients, and the teams—internal and external—that you put together to deliver those solutions, you have created a frame for your firm that will allow you to deliver your value!

Wouldn't it be great if you could explain your value to clients in a clear way? That's when your marketing materials will come in handy. Your marketing materials will describe your purpose, who you do serve, and how you deliver value.

THE eXchange™
Online Tool 7.2: Brainstorming the New Frame

Noble purpose, target market, needs, solutions, centers of influence, and value-delivering team, what a comprehensive list! For access to a step-by-step guide for defining your new frame, including additional brainstorming ideas for your team to tackle, go to the eXchange™ at youvebeenframed.clientwise.com.

 Just Say No to the Elevator Speech

Advisors often have an insatiable appetite for coming up with the perfect statement to provide when asked, "What do you do?" It's the proverbial elevator speech: how to pitch your company in a single sentence before the lift hits the tenth floor. "Hello, my name is Ray. I am a wealth advisor at Newco Wealth Management and we provide peace of mind." Ridiculous! The elevator speech worked in an era of sales, when advisors were pitching. Today, in the era of partnership, it usually falls flat.

While there are certainly times that you will need to be able to pitch your company quickly, I encourage you to think about how to best describe your noble purpose and the types of clients your firm is built

(Continued)

(Continued)

to serve. Yes, it's okay to be specific and authentic. You might even be surprised at the reaction you get from others, who are used to hearing the typical elevator pitch.

The elevator speech was, in many ways, based on capturing a client's attention (self-serving). Your authentic description of your company, grounded in your noble purpose and confident in your depiction of your ideal client, is more focused in how you are able to help the client (other directed). It is less about having a handy marketing statement and more about taking a genuine approach that is in alignment with your firm's values and capabilities. Focus on articulating your client's real needs and being client centered and client wise.

What's more, the elevator speech often stays right there in the elevator, whereas being authentic about who you serve and how you serve them will guide all that your company does. It will show up in your annual client reviews, team meetings, conversations with other professionals, hiring practices, and more. It will also show up throughout your marketing material, which will become clear when you engage in the next step of the reframing process: building your new frame.

CONCLUSION

Whether you answer the six questions related to defining your new frame in a daylong meeting with your team or flesh them out over a series of team meetings, this process will take some time and dedication, but it's worth it. If you engage in this process authentically, giving it the time and mental "open space" it deserves, the end result, honestly, will be magnificent.

You will have the words to convey to your clients the power of what you can do for them. You will be able to deliver services customized to their very needs, and, in return, your clients will develop a love for what you can do for them. They will trust you, appreciate you, and remain loyal to you. They will want to tell others about you, and they might even do a happy dance in your honor when they wake up in the morning.

NOTES

1. Erin Botsford, personal interview, March 10, 2015, transcript, p. 5.

2. The Botsford Group, "Botsford Financial Group—Founder's Message," video, 3:18, posted March 5, 2015, www.botsfordfinancial.com/index.php.

3. The Botsford Group, "About Us: Our Firm," accessed April 9, 2015, www.botsfordfinancial.com/our_firm.php.

4. Gregory Mech, personal interview, March 16, 2015, transcript, p. 2.

5. Ibid.

6. Ibid.

7. Rishiraj Ranawat, "Tesla Roadster: The Car of the Future?," Ozytive, February 28, 2013, www.ozytive.com/2013/02/28/tesla-roadster-the-car-of-the-future/.

8. Bradley Berman, "Henrik Fisker Resigns from Fisker Automotive," *Wheels* (blog), *New York Times*, March 13, 2013, http://wheels.blogs.nytimes.com/2013/03/13/henrik-fisker-resigns-from-fisker-automotive/?_r=0.

9. Gregory Mech, personal interview, March 16, 2015, transcript, p. 3.

10. Ibid., p. 6.

11. Ibid., p. 8.

CHAPTER **8**

Building Your
New Frame

Now that you know what your new frame is going to be—that is, you've defined your ideal clients, client needs, corporate solutions, professional network, and value statement in step 2 of the reframe process—you are ready to go about step 3: building your new frame (see Figure 8.1).

Building the new frame includes three key elements:

1. Reframing your team
2. Reframing yourself as a leader
3. Reframing your marketing assets

Every successful and sustainable reframe includes each of these parts.

First, you want to know how to best design your team. It's time to develop, build, adjust, tweak, and/or augment your team so you can deliver the wealth management services outlined in your new frame from step 2 of the reframing process.

The human capital is what is going to make your newly framed business "go." Remember, you may think you're in the wealth management business, but really, you're in the human capital business that

161

Figure 8.1 Reframe Step 3: Build Your Frame

delivers wealth management. Your team is integral to the delivery of your value proposition.

You start with building your team first because your team has the potential to provide valuable contributions to the new marketing materials you'll soon be creating, whether from a content, a design, or an administrative capacity. Your team is also likely to be featured in your marketing materials, so it's best to figure out what your team looks like now.

Advisors often believe they have their team in place. But start to think about the sustainability of growth. Is the team you have today the team you will need to deliver your newly framed wealth management services? How confident are you that you have built a strategic hiring plan that will get you where you are planning to go? Have you considered all of the capacity that you'll need to expand or adjust for, the new capabilities that you'll likely want to add and grow into, and the creativity that you believe is necessary to create the interdependency that you desire for the team to soar? It bears repeating that you need to consider each of these three parts: capacity considerations, capability and technical skills, and creativity in those others you'll need to make your firm grow exponentially.

Once your updated team has been put together, you will continue to build your new frame by assessing and reframing your own leadership skills to make them maximally effective. There are several behaviors, many of which will be covered in this chapter, that you can adopt to help you bring your team together to successfully deliver your reframed wealth management services.

With a strong team supporting your reframed organization, you and the team will be ready to co-create your marketing communications plan and strategy. Included in that marketing plan is the task of developing communications that can be delivered across five modes of communication—phone, mail, electronic media, in person, and third party. Here the focus will be on putting your new frame into evidence at each of the different points of contact through which your client sees you, your potential client meets you, and the professionals with whom you interact encounter you.

Remember, at this point, many advisors might just *tell* the team what they are building rather than involving them and encouraging them to share their best thinking and input. It will not be so if you are truly engaging in a team and leadership reframe. These reframes will have you valuing every team member's contribution and inviting them into the process of collaboration to meet common goals that advance your organization and the clients' goals, including the creation of your valuable marketing assets.

Together you can work to convey information on your new frame consistently across all media and points of interaction with others. Consistency, consistency, consistency! It is only through the consistent message you communicate to others that your reframe can occur effectively. That consistency needs to occur with you as a leader, with your team, and with all of your other trusted advisors—those professional advocates you are including as part of your extended wealth management team.

KEY CONCEPT

An essential part of the reframing process is your team. Not only do they deliver your firm's services to your clients, but they also are a source of information, insight, and (consistent!) messaging during the reframing process.

LONE RANGER TO LEADER™

The following may be the most important part of any chapter in this entire book. No matter what the stage of your business, whether you are a sole practitioner (*solopreneur*), you have built a successful team structure, or you are a partner in a larger firm, the journey toward developing powerful leadership skills is exactly that: a journey. For our industry to evolve and mature, we must together focus on building our own leadership skills as well as those of the leaders of tomorrow. It will take time and effort; it will involve adjustments, new behaviors, and new ways of thinking. But no longer will it be acceptable to go it alone; no longer will it be acceptable to move as a lone ranger.

The industry is in fact moving in the right direction. At ClientWise, we recently conducted a survey of more than 600 wealth management professionals to gauge whether they are on teams, and, if so, what these teams look like. In fact, 80 percent of those who responded indicated they were working in a team setting! Figure 8.2 shows some of the interesting results we learned from those respondents who were working on a team.

If we are going to be honest and authentic in our approach with clients when we are telling them that we'll be there through life transitions with them, then we need to lead effective teams that can deliver to our clients now and in the future. No one advisor can be there always and forever, whereas the team has depth and reliability that can be trusted to truly and consistently deliver.

So the journey of building your team is in large part the journey of transforming from lone ranger to leader. Many advisors get stuck playing the part of the lone ranger because for a long time, they were

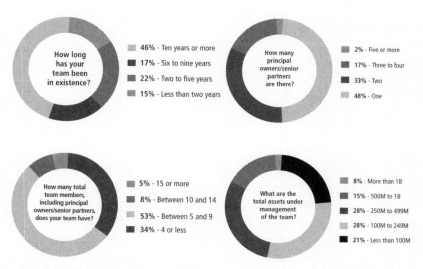

Figure 8.2 Team Makeup of More Than 300 Advisors (Answered by 323 Respondents)

the primary and sole practitioner who acquired the client, met with the client to build a plan, went back to the office, input all the data into the software, built the plan, went back to the client and represented the plan, and then went back to the office to put all the information to work and to manage the portfolio. Even those who years ago decided to build a team or even partner with other advisors to build a firm often find themselves working now in silos, alone, as lone rangers. For our industry to sustain itself and grow in providing true value for the client, we must evolve from lone rangers to leaders.

It's true that behind the scenes, these lone rangers may have had a support person doing a lot of the support-person kind of work, and yet in many cases the client really never saw any other professional other than that sole practitioner. Even in some financial advisory firms where there are already teams of professionals in place, there may still be a lead advisor operating with a lone ranger mind-set by hanging on to being the individual who's the primary contact for each client. This approach cannot sustain itself—in this model, the real loser is the client.

Unfortunately, a lone ranger can only manage a finite number of clients. What's more, true wealth management is too diverse to be handled by one professional. Trying to funnel all of the necessary wealth management tasks through one lone ranger–style lead advisor is likely doing a disservice to the client as the advisor struggles to meet the full breadth of important client demands.

INDUSTRY INSIGHT: BUILDING A TEAM FROM SCRATCH

Jonathan Beukelman, Managing Director of Wealth Management at the Beukelman Group, remembers when he first built a real team for his firm. The first big transition came when he moved from having a part-time virtual assistant that he shared with other firms to hiring his own in-house assistant. It meant investing extra money to hire someone to have in house, all the more so because Beukelman recruited a financial advisor, rather than an admin person, to do the job. The advisor had to take a leap of faith, as it was technically a step down on his career ladder, but Beukelman promised him that he was on a mission to grow the company and he would carry this advisor with him.[1]

(Continued)

(Continued)

Looking back, Beukelman has no regrets about the decision to hire his own assistant. It seemed to kick-start the beginning of something new, different, bigger, and better for his company. As Beukelman noted, "Once you get your own assistant, you feel internally that you actually have something."[2] With the support of an assistant, he found that he could communicate his value proposition better. Together, they could go deeper with clients and get more things done.

Today, Beukelman's firm has seven employees, and his initial employee—the advisor assistant—has grown with the firm. He has trained each new employee who has come on board, getting them up to speed, and he has run the business side of the firm for a long time, freeing up Beukelman to focus on other areas of the business.

To help clients get comfortable with the idea of working with a team, Beukelman and his firm are careful to share the team frame early on with prospects and new clients. They let clients know that there are multiple people on the team who will be working with the client in their particular areas of expertise. "For me, being able to communicate to clients, each individual person on the team and what their skill set is and how it comes together for the client, works pretty well," Beukelman explained.[3]

Beukelman takes pride in the fact that he does not have a team where each advisor simply works with his or her own set of clients in isolation; instead, his team tends to touch each client from the vantage point of their own expertise. Although the process is "not without challenges,"[4] Beukelman finds that as clients get to know the team, they typically learn who to reach out to in order to receive the specific support they require at a given time. According to him, the whole process runs pretty seamlessly.

The interesting thing is that even if every hiring decision that was made in putting together the team wasn't perfect, it all worked out in the end. Even if people did not land in the right spots when they first came on board the Beukelman Group, they were eventually moved to the area that best suited them.

Perhaps this is because Beukelman was smart enough to hire folks that had the right characteristics to fit into the vision he had for his firm's culture. He noted, "I had people that were extremely upbeat, that could work with clients on a consistent basis, and that would be there and committed to them."[5] As Beukelman interviewed people for his team, he looked for people who owned the things they were involved in. He wanted people who would take the business and the caretaking of clients' money as seriously as he did, and he found them.

At ClientWise, we have developed an extensive, four-part, 16-hour executive training program to help advisors grow from lone rangers to leaders and to help their teams evolve from lone ranger teams to true teams, not just work groups. (A *work group* is made up of staff members and/or contractors to whom the advisor hands off work; each member of the work group has individual goals that the advisor has set, but the group has not come together as a whole to mutually define success.) While all of material from the executive training program cannot be covered in this single chapter and will likely be the topic of a different book, I outline here fundamental aspects of that journey to help you build the new team frame in terms of who is on your team and how you can lead them most effectively.

 KEY CONCEPT

It's tempting to stick with a lone ranger approach to wealth management, but it's not necessarily in the clients' best interest for you to do so. Allowing a true team with diverse talents to handle the many tasks involved with effectively handling your clients' needs does not mean giving up control. Rather, sharing the work with your team's talented members will free you up to focus on your strengths and to build a stronger business.

Building Your Team

While defining your new frame in step 2, you took time to identify the professionals who would be on your *external team*; now it's time to get clear on what your *internal team* will look like.

If you are a solopreneur, you will be assessing whether you want or need to have an internal team and, if so, what it will look like. If you already stand at the head of a team in your organization, you can use this step to assess what changes, if any, need to be made to your team roster to be able to successfully and sustainably deliver on your new frame for your clients, now and in the future.

Here are some questions to consider as you engage in the brainstorming process of who you want and need on your new team:

■ Are you prepared and committed to building an internal team to successfully deliver your newly framed wealth management services, or will your external team be sufficient? How comfortable are you leading the team, or do you want to bring in someone else to be CEO, given your particular interests, strengths, and skill set?

- Are you willing to take the time and energy to truly lead an internal team, not just run a work group? How open are you to learning and improving new leadership skills so you can be the most effective leader you can be?

- What will you have to let go of to become the most effective leader for your team and your clients? How committed are you to developing the human capital on your team, codesigning professional development plans, and giving feedback and advice from a collaborative perspective? Are you ready and willing to do so? If not, what do you need to work through before you can move forward? While you may have imagined your work as a technician or as a financial advisor, how have you imagined yourself leading your wealth management firm?

- On a scale of 1 to 10 (1 being lowest functioning and 10 being highest functioning), how effective do you believe your current team is at achieving its goals? If less than 10, where could changes be made to improve team functioning? Personnel? Job roles? Leadership? Team culture?

By beginning to answer these questions, you will set the stage for understanding what kind of internal team makes the most sense for your firm. You will get clearer on your own willingness to lead a team and discover obstacles that may be standing in your way.

 Building a Team with the Right Capabilities

Although your team will have some unique requirements given your particular brand of wealth management, there are some foundational capabilities that every financial services team should have:

- Rainmaking
- Relationship management

- Technical capability
- Operational and administrative structure

At ClientWise, we recommend having the following three different kinds of advisors to help cover these capabilities. First, there is the *senior lead advisor,* who is dedicated primarily to rainmaking activities. This advisor's secondary role is as a strategic relationship manager, who only gets involved when a more senior partner is needed to help make a crucial decision.

Next, there is a *lead advisor,* whose primary role is to be a relationship advisor. Focused on complete client care, the lead advisor ensures that no accounts are leaving and that the team is delivering on the promises made to the client.

Last, there is a *service advisor,* who takes care of all follow-through and follow-up. He or she is essentially responsible for completing the work promised to the client. Sometimes the service advisor is front and center with clients, and other times he or she is behind the scenes, making sure all client information and paperwork is complete and in order.

It bears saying that as you undergo this process of building a team, not everyone has the same desire to step into the leadership role. If you happen to find yourself feeling uncertain about taking on that mantle, be honest with yourself. Talk to a coach credentialed by the International Coach Federation who specializes in working in the financial services industry or perhaps a mentor or respected other. Then give yourself time to determine whether it's a matter of moving past fear and potential obstacles or if you would simply prefer to spend your time engaging in the core of the financial services technical work rather than leading others who do so. You may also need to seriously consider how you are developing the future company and developing tomorrow's leaders, today. After all, if you are truly doing legacy work, leadership requires you to plan ahead for tomorrow. You deserve it. Your clients deserve it. And the firm you're building will have greater enterprise value.

Most of us have told the clients that we'll be there with them through their life transitions, so let's do that. It's simply not enough having a buy–sell agreement with another advisor down the block, with whom the client hasn't built a long-lasting relationship. It's not enough if you work in a large brokerage firm and you're counting on the office manager to distribute your client roster to other advisors in the office should something happen to you or you retire. You must plan, and you must plan ahead. Again, you deserve it. It's your life's work, after all. And, more important, your clients deserve it!

If in doubt regarding whether to build an internal team, explore what your goals for your company are and make some decisions about what is most important to you: doing work you love in the way you love to do it versus growing the company and its potential reach. Realistically, remaining a solopreneur (even with an external team to support you) may limit the number of clients you have and the depth of services you can offer. Yet this is your life and your business, and you get to make the call on how you want to shape and run both. Be conscious, get clear, and move forward in the way that is right for you. However you choose to structure your business, though, always keep in mind the promises you've made to clients and make sure you can follow through on them.

When you are ready to engage in building your internal team, check out the Coaching Corner exercise that follows.

 COACHING CORNER

Take some time to contemplate who you would like to have on your internal team. What skill sets, characteristics, and values are essential to each person's unique role and the overall team's success? In what ways may you need to restructure your current team members' job descriptions to be able to deliver your reframed wealth management services? What personnel changes, if any, do you anticipate needing to make to create your new team? Keep in mind that any well-balanced team will be able to win new clients, manage ongoing client relationships, engage in the technical aspects of the business, and operate and run the business.

THE eXchange™

Online Tool 8.1: A Guide to Defining Your High-Performing Team

Visit the eXchange™ for a 12-question guide to defining your unique high-performing team. Also visit the eXchange™ for a strategic hiring guide, sample job descriptions, and competency-based interview questions.

Leading Your Team

The design of your new team is just the first step in getting your team ready to deliver the new frame. It's also important to assess your own behaviors and make shifts where needed so that you are the most effective leader that you can be.

Make the Transition

At ClientWise, we invite advisors to enter into 10 transitions to grow into sophisticated leaders of highly effective teams. We have found that even those advisors already serving in leadership roles find that they grow when they put in the effort to move through these transitions. Here are the first three transitions. You will either believe these or you won't. If you don't believe these, you must reassess how prepared you are to truly build a strong team. You must believe:

- I am *part of a team* instead of a lone ranger.
- I see *team success* as more important than individual success.
- I am CEO or leader of the team, which means I must consistently engage in leadership activities.

It is interesting that the word *team* shows up three times in these statements, whereas *leadership* only appears once. It is not by accident that more emphasis is put on the group than the individual here. It is only by shifting from an individual perspective to the group or team perspective that an advisor may become a true leader.

In the old days, the leader had the mind-set of "boss." The top advisor, who was usually the biggest producer, drove the agenda and goals and told the "team" what to do and how to do it. In fact, this kind of structure isn't a team at all, it's a work group. That kind of work group doesn't fly in today's business landscape. Today the leader has to be capable of having the same mentality that he or she will ask of direct reports—a mentality that he or she is part of a team and that team success is more important than individual success.

It's all part of Total Team Leadership™, a term we've coined at ClientWise that is defined as follows:

> a leader and team who engage in the exchange of leadership among themselves in a manner that evokes meaningful contribution from every team member, showcases the strengths of each team member, and advances consistent and effective group decision making.

There is a true sense of inclusiveness in this new kind of financial services leader. Gone is the old structure of leader dictating down to direct reports; instead, we see the new structure in which the leader steps into the role of equal team member and then moves fluidly from this place into the leadership role of holding the vision, facilitating, and managing as needed, while empowering every member of the team to step up and lead. The leader needs to be able to move easily between his or her role as team member and team leader, and team members must be able to easily perceive that movement. It's the magic of team in the twenty-first century. This is especially true if you plan on bringing younger talent, the millennial, into the business. In the Total Team Leadership™ model, everyone has a voice and is expected to contribute to team goals.

 KEY CONCEPT

Effective teams are no longer work groups that unthinkingly follow the orders of a hierarchically superior "boss." Rather, team members are empowered contributors who have a voice in decision making and an investment in the group's success.

How does the advisor move through these three leadership transitions? Table 8.1 shows the different behaviors that the advisor can engage in to move through these transitions successfully.

Table 8.1 Ten Behaviors for Transitioning into a Total Team Leader

Transition	Behavior
I am part of a team instead of a lone ranger.	1. Regularly act as a member of the team instead of a leader. 2. Invite the members of the team to teach you so that shared learning occurs rather than simply top-down learning. 3. Share leadership with other members of the team. 4. Model attending to team goals and not just individual goals.
I see team success as more important than individual success.	5. Move easily and often from personally oriented activity to team productivity. 6. Align and merge your individual goals into team goals and encourage your team members to do the same. 7. Celebrate and reward team behavior and success.
I am CEO or leader of the team, which means I must consistently engage in leadership activities.	8. Model team behavior. 9. Encourage team participation. 10. Feel and evidence pleasure from helping to shape team achievement.

Allowing the importance of team to permeate all that you do will create an environment that helps your team coalesce, get inspired, and move forward to achieve the common goals of the team and the organization. The way to get from here to there is to commit to making the leadership *transitions* by diving into the associated *behaviors*.

THE eXchange™

Online Tool 8.2: Ten Steps to Leading a Highly Effective Team

Visit the eXchange™ for a printable checklist of the 10 leadership behaviors you can engage in to become the most effective leader for your team.

COACHING CORNER

Look at the 10 leadership behaviors featured in Table 8.1. Where are you currently doing well? Where do you see potential for your growth? Pick three behaviors you'd like to work on and add reminders to your calendar to work on each one for a month during the next three months. Rinse and repeat.

(*Continued*)

(*Continued*)

Also, in the eXchange™, you'll find a leadership self-assessment and an assessment for team members of their leader(s). The learning comes from the gaps, where the leader evaluates him- or herself and the team members evaluate his or her leadership ability.

Finding Common Purpose

As you are practicing and implementing Total Team Leadership™, you can set your team up for success by working with them to create a common intent, or common purpose, that will bind, motivate, and guide the group toward the desired future. At ClientWise, we define common intent and purpose as follows:

> an ambition that is significant in size, aspirational in scope, and possible to achieve that will serve your clients, yourselves, and your organization.

Common intent and purpose gets at the more inspiring ideas and aims that will drive your team's definition of wealth management, who the ideal client is, what solutions you offer, and what value you bring to the client. The most valuable common intents and purposes have an aim that is broader than the team itself and that includes an emotional component. Compare the following.

> To increase assets under management by X percent
>
> versus

> To help as many individuals as possible, including ourselves, to develop sufficient financial freedom to be able to engage in work or play driven only by their passion by the time they are 60

At ClientWise, we define our common intent and purpose as the following:

> Transforming the industry, one advisor at a time. For we believe that financial advising is noble work and when we make a positive impact in the life of one advisor, we make an impact positively on the lives of hundreds, for generations to come. When we impact 10,000 or more advisors and their firms, we've helped to transform

an industry for the better, creating a more mature and everlasting industry of noble workers.

Your team's common intent and purpose will get at why you do what you do. Another way of thinking of it is, what is the real purpose of your company besides making money? Simon Sinek, in his book *Start with Why*,[6] has created a terrific model for uncovering common purpose. Sinek argues that people don't buy what you do; they buy why you do it, which is an important point to have clear in the minds of everyone on your team. If your core values—if your driving passions—do not match up with those of your potential clients, you will have a much harder time bringing those clients into your fold.

In his TED talk, Sinek used the example of Dr. Martin Luther King Jr., who inspired people to follow him not because he told people what to do but because he told them what he believed. Sinek noted that 250,000 people showed up to listen to Dr. King's "I Have a Dream" speech, not his "I Have a Plan" speech. Further, they made the often lengthy trip to hear him speak not for Dr. King, but for themselves.[7]

You can foster the creation of a common intent and purpose by doing the following:

1. Start, encourage, and continue the conversation to set common intent and purpose.
2. Ensure that the common intent and purpose are large enough and aspirational enough to both bond and motivate the team at a deep level.
3. Engage team members to continue to connect with and commit to the team's common intent and purpose.
4. Model connecting to and acting in response to the team's common intent and purpose.

Common intent and purpose reflect why teams are actually created. Teams come together to do work that is larger than an individual, where collective energy and capacity combine to achieve something that an individual could or would never do alone. Common intent and purpose also make it easy for team members individually and collectively to move in the same direction, support one another, and serve clients at the highest level.

Common intent and purpose not only work to motivate your team and help them stay clear on the team's reason for being, they can also serve as great filters when you are hiring new team members to make sure they are a good fit. They also act as useful filters for determining what kind of clients you will work with because your ideal clients will value what you do and why, as encapsulated in your common intent and purpose.

KEY CONCEPT

Common intent and purpose will pull your current team together and help you attract and retain clients and new team members who share your vision and values.

REFRAMING YOUR MARKETING COLLATERAL

You've reframed your team and your own leadership style to help you lead your reframed team as effectively as possible. With these areas reframed, you are ready to create the marketing materials needed to effectively and consistently communicate your new frame to the world: to current clients, potential clients, other professionals, and more. These materials will be based on the frame you have defined previously in step 2: your ideal client, client needs, client solutions, professional network, and value statement.

Think Marketing Assets

The thing about a reframe is that to make it stick, you need to educate people about it while consistently communicating it. So as exciting as it may be that you have developed a new frame that caters to your clients' needs and your own interests and skill sets, it will be relatively meaningless if you don't put it into evidence across your marketing materials.

You have a new story to tell; your marketing materials need to reflect the new story so others can learn and understand it. You also need the assets that you can share with your loyal client advocates and the professional advocates who will tell your story. You must arm them with the tools and resources to make their jobs easier in supporting you and your team.

Think of your marketing materials as assets. It's a term advisors are familiar with, and I use it to help remind us of how valuable our marketing materials are to our businesses' growth, success, and sustainability. Consider some of the ways in which the term *asset* is defined, then consider these within the context of your marketing materials:

- "A resource with economic value that an individual, corporation or country owns or controls with the expectation that it will provide future benefit."[8]
- "Something valuable that an entity owns, benefits from, or has use of, in generating income."[9]
- "A useful or valuable quality, skill, or person."[10]

That last definition gets to the heart of the competitive advantage that your marketing assets can create for you. Most advisors are not marketers or branders; if you rally your own team and/or bring in marketing experts to help you brand your firm, you will not only stand out among your competitors but also increase your ability to win clients.

In sum, your marketing materials are nothing short of valuable assets for your organization. You need to invest in them—through time, brainpower, and money—and then, if you execute well, you can expect a return on that investment.

Will your marketing assets have value per se? As you can guess, my answer to that question is yes. In the near term, your marketing assets are an integral mode of acquiring new clients, keeping current clients satisfied, and providing your professional network with the communication tools for making introductions to you from new clients. If your marketing materials help you win engagements with your ideal clients and retain current clients, they are providing you with economic value in the form of dollars those new clients bring in.

KEY CONCEPT

Your marketing materials are assets that need to describe your organization's reframe consistently. Invest time, talent, and resources into these essential tools for informing your potential clients and partners about who you are, what you do, and what you stand for.

In the longer term, your up-to-date, well-framed marketing assets can help you to sell your company successfully at the appropriate time, should you choose to do so, because they are your brand in evidence. They are an essential tool to continually attract your ideal client so you can continue to provide your firm's unique definition of wealth management services.

How many resources (time, money, and effort) are you willing to spend on your marketing assets if you know that they will bring you a high multiple in returns?

The Five Modes of a Marketing Communications Plan

It's a shift for some advisors to imagine putting a lot of energy into branding or marketing their firm. They may prefer to be out in the field meeting clients, back in the office doing the research, putting together the financial plan, or creating the client presentation. They may not have ever realized how powerful their marketing assets can be, or they may know how important they are and have just not found the time to keep them up to date.

Either way, to successfully engage in the reframe, advisors need to make it a priority to give their marketing materials an update or an overhaul. Even those advisors who already have excellent marketing assets will likely need to look into redoing and updating their materials to reflect their new frame. Designing new marketing materials is a key step in the reframing process.

Marketing assets exist across five media, as described in Table 8.2.

As you can see, there are a lot of ways to reach your ideal clients and attract them to your new brand of wealth management services. Instead of jumping into a big marketing campaign across all of these media (can you say "overwhelming"?), I encourage you to create instead a presentation that includes the key elements of your new frame. This can serve as a central resource for guiding the development of any future marketing campaigns as well as an internal training tool for your newly framed team. We call this the *capability deck*.

Creating Your Capability Deck

If you are or ever were in financial services in a corporate or large organizational setting, chances are that you have made hundreds of pitch

Table 8.2 Five Major Modes of Marketing Assets

Asset Type	Definition	Examples
Electronic	Any material that gets posted or distributed digitally to convey your frame and attract your ideal clients	Website Social media Blog Videos E-mails E-newsletter
Old-fashioned "snail mail" (print)	Any print material that gets sent to individuals via traditional mail to convey your frame and attract your ideal clients	Newsletter Annual report Financial plans Client statements Invoices Holiday greetings Special offers & announcements
Phone	Any devices used to ensure that the conversations you have with individuals over the phone convey your frame and attract ideal clients; these often come in the form of scripts that you and your team follow when engaging in phone conversations	Phone talking points and scripts for ■ speaking with potential clients ■ onboarding new clients ■ conducting phone check-ins with clients
In person	Any materials you can use or give when meeting with potential or current clients in person to convey your frame and attract and retain your ideal clients	Talking points and scripts for ■ new client meeting ■ client review Company brochure Business cards Financial plan Investment reports
Third party	Any materials you provide to your advocates, both clients and professionals, to make it easy for them to accurately frame you for potential clients and attract them to your business	Advocate brochure Referral postcards Company fact sheet Conversation scripts (phone and in person)

books in your career, maybe even thousands. It's the PowerPoint presentation with your firm's logo stamped all over it, a matching color scheme, lists of bulleted facts and figures, attention-getting quotations, colorful graphs and charts, a company vision statement, service descriptions, client promises, and clip art images that whiz onto the screen. It's a sales tool. Pitch books are old fashioned.

Instead, create a capability deck that is fully client oriented. Make it useful. Create it in a way that it will convey your new frame. Make it the most powerful presentation that you ever create, with well-constructed and highly meaningful information for helping you communicate to clients and other professionals why you do what you do, who you do it for, and how you do what you do that is unique and distinguishing. The reframe capability deck is your opportunity to pull together all of the market research and analysis that you conducted during the ClientWise Conversation™ (step 1 of the reframe) and while defining your new frame (step 2). It's your storyboard, so to speak: a springboard for communicating your new frame to clients (step 4) and your network of advocates (step 5).

Your capability deck should cover the following topics:

- Why you do what you do
- Who your firm is built to serve
- Known needs of your clients
- Unknown needs of your clients
- Solutions you provide to your clients
- Your unique, client-outcome-oriented wealth management process
- Your team of trusted professionals (internal and external)
- What the client could expect if he or she was to work with your firm, the process for becoming a client, and how the client will be served after signing on

If you have more than one ideal client type, separate these out, so each deck reflects one type's own unique needs, solutions, wealth management process, and trusted advisors. Consider whether your wealth management process has to be adjusted on the basis of the ideal client type. For example, your wealth management process would look different for professional athletes who earn income early in their careers that may need to last a lifetime compared to corporate executives who plan on working until age 55. You'll want your presentation to reflect those differences. Although the core of your presentation will likely remain consistent across client types, you may need to customize certain parts of it, such as your client engagement model.

As you build your capability deck, look back at the frame you created in step 2 of the reframing process, including any work you may have generated when completing Online Tool 7.2: Brainstorming the New Frame. Refine it and revise it as needed, including it in the capability deck to accurately convey your new frame. Once it is complete, you can use the capability deck internally to guide how you build all of your new marketing assets and as a tool to educate and frame yourself and your firm in front of clients, prospective clients, and other trusted advisors. It will also be an outstanding training tool for every member of your team.

KEY CONCEPT

A *capability deck* is a client-oriented marketing tool that conveys not only what you can do for the client but why you do what you do, who you do it for, and how what you do is like what no one else does. It is an excellent tool for communicating your reframe.

Organizing Your Marketing Campaign

With your capability deck created, you will have a central resource to guide your new marketing campaign, which should be executed across the five marketing modes in Table 8.2: electronic, mail, phone, in person, and third party. To keep your marketing campaign manageable and ensure a professional product, consider hiring a marketing firm or outside expert to help you create and implement it. Some financial services firms are well positioned to take care of the marketing themselves—if so, you probably already know who you are. If in doubt, interview other marketing professionals who can help you. At a minimum, you will learn something in the process; at a maximum, you will find support for your firm if you ultimately decide that you need or desire it.

THE eXchange™

Online Tool 8.3: Marketing Firms to Help You Build Your Brand

We've created a resource group of marketing firms that specialize in the financial services industry. Go to the eXchange™ for a list of firms that you might find useful.

As you begin to put your marketing strategy and plan together, consider the order in which you should create your new assets. Which are essentials that must be created before you can launch the new frame, and which assets can be added later on or as you go? For example, a good website and business cards are a must at the start of the new frame, whereas referral postcards for your advocates and holiday greetings can be created down the line. You may find yourself creating talking points or scripts for phone and in-person conversations on an as-needed basis—before the next scheduled client review or your next lunch date with one of your advocates, for example.

When you have decided which campaigns you want to tackle first, give each one a name and list the following details for each:

- Expected payoff/ROI
- Target market, niche, and ideal client profile
- Possible offer(s)
- Relevant messages
- Delivery options
- Who on the team is involved
- Start and end dates of the campaign

Table 8.3 shows a sample campaign.

Table 8.3 represents just one of the infinite possibilities for how a firm may choose to construct their marketing strategy and plan. In fact, this is an example of just one particular campaign among what could be multiple campaigns to help target different types of ideal clients. For example, the financial services firm represented in Table 8.3 might also include pediatric physician assistants and pediatric nurse practitioners on their ideal client list, which might require two additional customized marketing campaigns.

Table 8.3 Marketing Campaign Example

Campaign	Expected Payoff/ ROI	Target Market	Ideal Client Profile	Possible Offer(s)	Relevant Messages	Delivery Options
Pediatrician outreach	75–100 client leads generated	Physicians	Pediatricians w/ practices ≤ 5 years old	■ One free session of wealth management counseling ■ Complimentary financial plans for physician's family ■ Link to a downloadable checklist: *Wealth Management Issues for the Pediatrician Who Owns an Independent Practice*	■ We have been successfully working with physicians for over 15 years to mitigate risk and build sustainable wealth management strategies. ■ We have spoken to more than 250 pediatricians' offices nationwide to understand their needs, and we have developed targeted solutions to address them.	■ Quarterly e-newsletter to existing database of 2,500 physicians ■ Postcard mailer to 2,000 pediatricians' offices ■ Sponsor a lunch at national pediatricians' conference in May

What will your marketing strategy and plan look like? Which campaigns will it involve and how can these campaigns be executed? As you contemplate the execution of your marketing strategy, plan to prioritize campaigns and phase them in over time to ensure you and your team can successfully manage them and get the most out of them. Brainstorm with abandon; plan with reality in mind; execute with consistency; and enjoy watching the very real results as your new ideal clients come in the door over time.

 THE eXchange™

Online Tool 8.4: Marketing Campaign Organizer™

It's time to create your marketing campaign. Visit the eXchange™ to download and print a Marketing Campaign Organizer™ that will allow you to outline your next marketing campaign, including target market, ideal client profile, possible offers, relevant messages, delivery options, who is involved, start and end dates, and expected ROI.

CONCLUSION

The creation of marketing assets is admittedly a big task and will take time. Have a plan and engage others to help you create milestones for all of the assets your firm would like to build to reflect your new frame or enhance your previous frame, based on what you've now co-created as a team. For those tempted to succumb to the mental block of "I can't do it!" I offer the following advice.

First, you've got a team now; enlist them in working toward your common intent and purpose.

Second, although compliance is a very real consideration when it comes to how you can legally present your firm in your marketing materials, move ahead by investigating the rules of what you can and can't do and consult an expert when needed. Instead of leading with "I can't," start with what it is that you really do and stand for, then partner with those in the compliance area to help your message come alive in a way that clearly and authentically frames what you do.

Last, engage the professional advice and guidance of a marketing consultant or hire an expert to work in house to help you do the custom writing, designing, and publishing that will be required. Your message to your firm's ideal client, distributed across multiple media, must not get stale.

While this may currently be problematic for advisors affiliated with any of the large brokerage firms today, this will need to change in time. The new rules for marketing today, called *inbound marketing* or *content marketing,* mean that if you want to be known as an expert, you must consistently publish your content so you are viewed as relevant.

For those of you who are able to do this now, get more serious about how you can put yourself forward as an expert in your field and among those your firm is truly built to serve. Build a terrific marketing organization that communicates all that you do, so you can get to serving many others for generations to come.

When excellent marketing is not just window dressing but opens the door to excellent client support, our whole industry moves forward. Invest in creating authentic marketing assets, take the time to build the right team for your particular kind of wealth management, and find the courage and patience to push your own leadership skills ever higher, into the realm of "we are a team." In doing so, the frame that you and your team have so consciously created and constructed for your clients will become a living reality that inspires others in the industry—and even beyond—to do the same.

NOTES

1. Jonathan Beukelman, personal interview, March 13, 2015, transcript, p. 6.
2. Ibid.
3. Ibid.
4. Ibid.
5. Ibid., p. 7.
6. Simon Sinek, *Start with Why: How Great Leaders Inspire Everyone to Take Action* (New York: Portfolio, 2011).
7. "Start with Why—How Great Leaders Inspire Action," YouTube video, 18:01, from a TEDxPugetSound talk, posted by TEDx Talks, September 28, 2009, www.youtube.com/watch?v=u4ZoJKF_VuA.
8. *Investopedia: Dictionary,* s.v. "Asset," accessed April 2, 2015, www.investopedia.com/terms/a/asset.asp.
9. *BusinessDictionary.com,* s.v. "Asset," accessed April 2, 2015, www.businessdictionary.com/definition/asset.html.
10. *Cambridge Dictionaries Online,* s.v. "Asset," retrieved April 2, 2015, http://dictionary.cambridge.org/dictionary/british/asset.

PART III

Now What?

CHAPTER 9

Teaching Others How to Frame You

Renewing Relationships

The preparation for your reframe is complete. You've collected data from your clients and professional network; you've used it, along with your team brainstorm, to inform how you want to define your new frame; and you've built your new frame by revamping your team and creating your new marketing assets. Your new frame is now ready to share with your clients. This is step 4 of the reframing process (see Figure 9.1). At ClientWise, we refer to it as *renewing relationships* because you are not just telling your client about your new frame, you are focusing on strengthening your relationship with the client more than ever as you make it clear that the reframe is based on all you've learned from your clients and is there to help you serve the client better.

You may be thinking, "But I've just tweaked our brand—why do I need to make a production of the rollout?" First, give yourself and your team the credit everyone deserves. After all, it took a great deal

189

Figure 9.1 Reframe Step 4: Renew Relationships

of effort to commit to and follow through on this very important work, and you all deserve recognition for that work. Second, you may have a good handle on what you do and what you've always done, but remember that your clients may not have always seen you in the frame you think you have for yourself. If nothing else, reaching out now gives you a reason to renew your relationship with your clients while ensuring that you and your clients are currently on the same page, looking at the same frame.

As with each of the previous steps of the reframe, step 4 involves a process imbued with intent. This step's focus is on educating the client on your new frame within the context of renewing your relationship with the client. You will be teaching your client about your new frame, but doing so in a way that is grounded in the client relationship and your partnership together.

It is not a top-down approach of "Hey, client, this is our new brand!" but instead a partnering approach that began when you asked for client feedback during the ClientWise Conversation™ (step 1) and is now logically progressing as you return to the client with an update on what you've built after collecting client feedback. In Figure 9.2, compare and contrast these two approaches to delivering the new frame.

In step 4, as throughout the reframing process, the client will always be at the center of what you do. This process began with clients when you collected data from them, and it continued with clients when you analyzed their feedback and used it to inform how you wanted to define your new frame. You also spent a great deal of time envisioning who your ideal clients would be, and now you are returning to your clients to reinvigorate your relationships with a check-in and the positive news on all you have been building to better serve them.

It's all about authentically renewing your relationship with the client—sharing with the client what you've learned from client

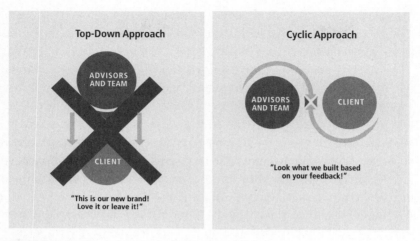

Figure 9.2 Sharing the New Frame with Your Clients

feedback, informing him or her why you are designing the firm the way you now are, and inviting the client to engage with you as you grow into a new and even better version of your organization.

KEY CONCEPT

When presenting the new frame, plan to renew your relationship with your client, whose feedback shaped your current frame and whose future feedback will influence changes yet to come.

There are three major aspects to renewing the client relationship: presenting the new frame to your existing clients at an in-person meeting, actively transitioning your existing clients to working with your new and improved team, and acquiring new clients for your new company. It all begins with the Client Renewal Conversation.

DELIVERING THE FRAME, DELIVERING THE FIRM

You've rebuilt your marketing assets, and you now have a capability deck that showcases with whom you work, what you provide your clients in terms of solutions and value, and why. Now you're ready to set up meetings with your existing clients to share your new frame with them. You are going to have a Client Renewal Conversation in which you reframe yourself with clients who have known you a certain way for so long.

How long have your clients known you, and how were you framed when they first met you, perhaps long ago? How much has your firm evolved since then, and how much has your own role changed? You will be having the Client Renewal Conversation with existing clients who already know you as a firm—and perhaps have known you a particular way for some time now. This conversation is about getting these individuals comfortable with and even excited about your reframed firm and the potential value it can bring to them.

If you recall how to get the most out of the ClientWise Conversation™, you will likely see some similarities between the best ways to approach the ClientWise Conversation™ and to have the Client Renewal Conversation. Here are the important elements of the Client Renewal Conversation:

- *Start by inviting your clients to meet in person for the Client Renewal Conversation.* It's easier to make a connection when face-to-face than over the phone, and this typically provides you more space and time to connect with the client.

- *Come from a position of strength* when you invite your clients to meet and when you speak to them at the meeting itself. Explain how you are a learning organization and always working to improve your service to clients. You're excited to share with them some ways you plan to better serve your clients and get their continued feedback.

- *Plan to meet with each of your clients to introduce your new frame to them.* Think about which clients you need to meet with personally versus which clients your team members may be best positioned to meet with. For example, if you have expanded your team to include a lead advisor who will be handling certain relationships as the primary advisor, it may make sense for that advisor to meet with those clients. Consider issues like how comfortable you expect your client to be in meeting with you versus other team members, and decide on the basis of your expectations for success.

- *Bring key members of your team to the meeting.* Whereas you attended the ClientWise Conversation™ solo, so as not to overwhelm or "team up" on the client, the Client Renewal Conversation is a good time to introduce your clients to any new members of your team. But get your clients' permission to bring additional people; if they would prefer to meet only with you, respect that and plan to transition them over to your new team in the future. As you bring team members to the meeting, you may not be taking as much of a lead as you had in the past. You're allowing others to share leadership and take ownership of the meeting.

- *Showcase your new frame* by walking the clients through your capability presentation. I call this process "delivering the firm." Share with the clients who your new and improved firm is built to serve, how you serve them, and why you serve them. Answer for them the following questions: What are your solutions and how will these meet the needs of your clients? What is your unique wealth management process? What value do you bring to the client? Who is on your team to make all of this possible?

- *Be consistent and clear as you deliver your message.* If you want people to think differently about your firm, you have to explain your new frame in a way that is understandable and consistent throughout. Make sure that your words and visual aids at the meeting all match up with one another and the new frame.

- *Highlight your new team and your own role in the new frame.* If your role has changed in the new frame, let your clients know what new responsibilities you will be carrying versus delegating and why. Introduce your new team members and let the clients know that these changes will allow you to deliver the full value you've promised for the benefit of the clients. Ask the clients for permission to bring team members onto their account.

- *Listen to your clients' reactions and feedback.* Take the time to observe your clients' reactions to the new frame; ask for questions, feedback, and input. Your relationship with each client is a partnership, so clients' voices really matter.

KEY CONCEPT

The Client Renewal Conversation consists of scheduling in-person meetings with your clients to showcase your new frame. Plan on opening from a position of strength, being clear and consistent in your message, highlighting the new team and new roles in the frame, and listening to client feedback and reactions.

As much as you are talking during the Client Renewal Conversation, you are also coming from a place of curiosity and listening. This is an opportunity to show clients that you listened to them during the ClientWise Conversation™ and that your new frame incorporates what you learned. It's also an important time to gauge your client's reaction to your new frame and respond to it.

As during the ClientWise Conversation™, it's important to be open to feedback rather than defensive. Respond to client concerns with curiosity and interest and be prepared to listen for what the client is really saying (e.g., "Tell me more." "Can you say more about that?" "I'm really glad you took the time to share your thoughts on this.").

It can be helpful, too, to redirect the client to the benefits of your new frame, underscoring or reviewing the ways in which you anticipate your new frame can bring the client greater wealth, offer the client greater support, save the client time, and so on. I've often found that as long as the reframe will benefit clients (i.e., you can answer what I call the WIIFM question, or "What's in it for me?"), they are fine with the new and improved firm. After all, clients do want to see that you are growing, improving, and learning: Expansion on your part benefits them.

By being intentional in your communications with clients and even explaining how your reframe is grounded in integrity—reflective of your firm's strengths and passions—you will help to build trust with clients and, with trust, loyalty.

As you engage in the Client Renewal Conversation, plan as well to clarify the answer to the question, How will you be able to deliver on the promise made to clients that you will be here for them through life transitions? You can't live forever, which means you may not actually be there for your clients through all of life's transitions; your team, however, can.

During the Client Renewal Conversation, you can highlight for clients the growth that you have planned for your team to ensure your firm's sustainability. Another way of saying this is that you've made strategic hiring decisions and you've got a solid succession plan in place. That should be reassuring news to your client.

KEY CONCEPT

Remember that there are two sides to the Client Renewal Conversation: It is just as much about listening as about talking. Keep an open mind to your clients' reactions and feedback.

Renewing relationships, on a larger scale, should really be an ongoing process. It's a ritual that you'll want to build into your interactions with clients, being sure to check in with them in this way every 18 months more formally, delivering the firm with every client interaction and every client review. Consistency! Consistency! In this way, as your organization continues to evolve, you can keep your clients up to date on the ways in which you can better serve them, not just today but tomorrow, too.

In fact, I encourage you to approach your clients from a perspective of discovery each and every time you interact with them. How have their lives changed? Things happen all the time in people's lives. Clients buy new pieces of real estate. They sell one company and buy another. They inherit some money they didn't know they were going to inherit. They take vacations, their children go off to college, or they check their parents into nursing homes. Really know their families, their children, and their heirs.

While you are discovering things about your clients, you should also be revealing the changes happening in your firm. As an organization, you are always changing. Maybe you have hired a certified financial planner or added some new technology. Maybe you've launched some new services or tweaked your processes. The client needs to know about these things; keep him or her informed. And, of course, do so in a way that is consistent with your new frame. As things at your firm change, explain how and why these changes support the value that you continually strive to deliver to clients. Through this consistent messaging, you will reinforce your clients' ability to think of your firm in the new and improved way.

Things change in your clients' lives, and things change at your company. By approaching your clients with curiosity about what is going on in their lives, you will also pave the way for you to share what has changed lately at your organization. Stay sharp by regularly renewing the relationship with your clients.

KEY CONCEPT

The Client Renewal Conversation is not a one-time event. Change is ever occurring with your clients and with you. Check in regularly so you can keep up with your clients' needs and they can stay aware of the services you offer.

COACHING CORNER

With which clients do you need to set up meetings to have the Client Renewal Conversation? Plan to go back to all of the clients whom you value. If any of these individuals no longer meet your ideal client profile, prepare for the difficult conversation in which you and they work together to determine whether your firm continues to be the right one for them and, if not, what firm might be a better fit. Otherwise, enjoy the journey of delivering your firm to your valued clients.

INDUSTRY INSIGHT: PREPARING TO WORK WITH THE HEIRS OF YOUR CLIENTS

In 2009, Diane Doolin, senior vice president of the Doolin Group at Morgan Stanley and a *Barron's* "Top 100 Women" financial advisor, knew she wanted to differentiate herself from other financial advisors. She was interested in how she could serve not just her clients but their whole families. Doolin decided to attend a presentation on the topic of passing on values as well as money, designed for business founders and their heirs as well as professional advisors. When she arrived, she was surprised to find that the room was filled with business owners and wealthy families but no advisors aside from herself and her business partner.

What surprised Doolin even more, however, was the moment when one of the speakers, Roy Williams, president and founder of the Williams Group, shared that 70 percent of all wealth transfers fail. It was an "aha!" moment for Doolin, who suddenly realized that advisors knew how to manage money well, execute estate planning documents well, and transfer money in a tax-efficient way. The money got to the heirs. It was within families that problems occurred because of lack of trust and communication, heirs not being prepared, and family values not being shared in conversations.

Doolin thought, "As financial planners, we have the perfect plan in place, [and] the returns are terrific. But all that being said, what if after the money is passed on, everything falls apart? What are we really doing of value here [. . .] if it ends with this generation?" Doolin was inspired to do better by her clients.

She met with Roy Williams and his partner, Vic Preisser, an executive coach and mentor to heirs with the Williams Group, who shared the highlights of what they had learned over the years in serving high-net-worth families. At first, Doolin was excited at the prospect of using the information she was gaining to better serve her clients and their families and, in turn, her business. Before long, however, she realized that what she was discovering was "way too big" to keep it from the industry.

The result is the Institute for Preparing Heirs®, a training company (of which Doolin is a founding director) that serves financial advisors who work with high-net-worth multigenerational families. The Institute offers advisors a variety of tools and resources to help advisors better serve their high-net-worth families, including white papers, family conversation-starter checklists, family meeting resources, marketing resources, webinars, and training videos. As the Institute has coalesced and grown, Doolin has been in the thick of it, testing new tools and resources as they are developed.

When asked how her financial advisory practice has benefited from the time she has given to the Institute, Doolin explained how it helps her in every conversation she has with clients. It deepens her relationship with clients and opens up the door for her to work with their children, parents, and other family members. In describing the "inheritance conversation" that she has with clients, Doolin noted, "This conversation is, with the highest intention, a relationship builder. It can impact your business in a positive, relationship-oriented way. You attract really nice people when you have good intentions for their family; it's a whole different way of doing things."

Doolin has seen quantitative benefits as well. After running her annual Client University, with topics such as "How, What, and When Do I Tell the Kids?" "Your Estate Plan Is Set, But Is Your Family Prepared?" and, for women, "Assuming the Mantle of Family Financial Leadership," Doolin received a phone call from a woman who wanted her to set up a family foundation for her. She was interested in working with Doolin because of her focus on involving the family. Today, this particular client relationship is at $40 million, and Doolin anticipates that it could go much higher.

(Continued)

(Continued)

Doolin suggests that advisors think of the opportunity to assist clients in transferring their wealth to families as a chance to keep up with the times by reinventing themselves. She recalled how in the past advisors had to reframe themselves from being transactional brokers who bought and sold stocks to "advice givers" or professional advisors regarding asset allocation. Over time, advisors became "trusted advisors"; today, she believes that the new shift for those in the industry is to become "the trusted family advisor." It's time, Doolin said, for the advisor to look not just at Mr. and Mrs. Jones, but at their whole family as the client.

TRANSITIONING CURRENT CLIENTS TO THE TEAM FRAME

During the Client Renewal Conversation, you will introduce your new team to the client, whether in person or through your capability deck. The team reframe, like so much of the reframe process, will need to be ongoing. You've got to do some additional transition work to help the client get comfortable working with your new or revamped team.

The next time you interact with the client, plan to continue the discussion you began during the Client Renewal Conversation in which you let the client know you've built out or revamped your team and why, grounding your answers in how the team can benefit the client. Continue to communicate to get the client's permission to bring other team members into your work with the client, and then start getting your team members involved so they are sharing responsibility for the client.

 KEY CONCEPT

Remember that the Client Renewal Conversation is also about your team. It provides the opportunity to talk about the talents and services the team members have to offer and to introduce them in person as conversation participants.

On a practical level, as you move forward, you should never be on a client review alone again. Bring other team members to the calls, and slowly but surely you will find that your client will develop trust for the rest of your team, not just you. Share leadership, allowing others on the team to provide advice and guidance.

Here's where the three types of advisors described in Chapters 4 and 8—senior, lead, and service advisors—come in. Make sure that other members of the team are participating in a way that the client can see; over time, as your team achieves successes, the client will have greater faith in it. In sum, have a plan, be consistent, and never be the only one conducting the client review again.

When it comes to reframing your new team that delivers wealth management for your firm, you will likely have three kinds of clients:

1. *Those who trust you inherently and are excited about the new and improved firm.* They are enthusiastic about the new capabilities, the new capacity, and better client service you'll be offering. Heck, many of these types of clients would do anything you suggested, so if you're on board, they're on board.

2. *Those who will need some time to embrace these changes and improvements.* You'll need to calibrate how long you're willing to wait for them to transition with you.

3. *Those who, no matter what, will only work with you.* There are two types of these clients: those who you will likely continue to work with, and those who will likely not make the journey to the new and improved firm.

As you engage in the transition process, it will become clear who is who. Be grateful for those who trust you inherently and are excited about the process; take your time with those who seem open to the team idea but are not as fast to trust and transition. As for those clients who have framed you as the only one they should be dealing with, you will have to decide how to reconcile this with your new frame. Are you willing to stay tied to your old role with this client for their business, or is it time to let the client go? You get to make the choice.

INDUSTRY INSIGHT: GETTING CLIENTS COMFORTABLE WORKING WITH THE TEAM

Kelly Campbell, founder and CEO of Campbell Wealth Management, shared the story of how he successfully transitioned his clients to working with his team many years

(*Continued*)

(Continued)

ago. In particular, he recounted what it was like to remove himself from review meetings with clients.

At first, Campbell admits, he wasn't as intentional as he could have been when transitioning himself out of meetings. Instead, he casually suggested to a couple of his employees that perhaps they could attend the review meetings for two clients that week. He was sure to join the meetings for a time, but then he departed.

This worked all right, but, over time, Campbell became much more intentional about laying the groundwork for the process and would explain to clients early on that they would be meeting with his service team for review meetings. He would let them know that he had built this team expressly to deliver reviews to the clients, to give them the best service possible, and so they would always have someone to talk to, given that he is typically in meetings all day.

Today, occasionally, a client will ask Campbell if he can pop into the meeting, and he does. But he finds that all he needs to do now is say hello or answer a couple of questions and then he can depart.

This has all been part of a larger team reframe that Campbell undertook early on. As he brought in new clients, he introduced all of his team members, then explained his role in business development, certain team members' roles in service, and other team members' roles in managing client portfolios. With this clear communication up front, Campbell finds that clients are comfortable working with the team, and the firm is set up for success to deliver the best service possible to its clients.

Campbell suggested that advisors undertaking the team reframe learn to trust the way they've designed their team and carry that confidence forward when informing clients about the team. "You've got to trust the system," Campbell stated, "and you've got to tell that to clients. 'This is the way our program works.'"[1]

When asked how he handles it when a client is unwilling to work with others on the team besides him, Campbell explained that his firm won't take that person as a client. He noted that this is rarely the case—and often, when it is, other issues are going on as well—but he is clear that his clients have to be comfortable working with his team.

Campbell believes that his clients undoubtedly benefit from the team approach. He noted, "They get a dedicated service team . . . they get their questions answered thoroughly and much more quickly."[2] In addition, they get a financial plan conducted for them once a year, something that Campbell couldn't offer if he worked as a lone ranger. Campbell believes firmly in the importance of the financial plan and its ability to help the firm and the client make sure they are on track and headed in the right direction. It's just one of the many areas of value that he can offer to his clients because of his team frame.

ACQUIRING NEW CLIENTS FOR YOUR NEW FRAME

With the time you've spent helping your existing clients understand your new frame and the energy you've invested in renewing those relationships, you are well on your way to making the transition to your new and improved company. From here, you have the freedom and opportunity to acquire new clients—those ideal individuals whom you so consciously identified earlier in the reframing process.

If you've already had the Client Renewal Conversation with your existing clients, chances are that you'll find it relatively easy to frame your firm for prospective and new clients. These are the easiest individuals of all for whom to frame your company, as this is the very first time they are meeting you.

Simply use all of the materials you've created to communicate your new frame—capability deck, updated website, introductory video, documented engagement models, and the like—to share with your prospects and new clients what your firm does, who you do it for, why you do it, and what your team looks like.

With such a clear and conscious process in place, you are likely to discover that the right clients start being attracted to your firm, almost as if by magic. Of course, with you and your team having invested hours of effort in this process so far, it's not magic at all. It is, however, the growth of the seeds of change you have planted.

At ClientWise, we teach advisors a process to guide them from attracting clients to acquiring clients to integrating them into their firm. It's called the 3 Stages of the Client Acquisition Process™: Stage 1, Campaign Management; Stage 2, Opportunity Management; and Stage 3, New Client Integration. Figure 9.3 provides a snapshot of this process.

In Stage 1, you focus on generating, managing, and converting leads. As you move through this stage, be clear about the most effective ways that you, your team, and your designated rainmakers can generate new leads for the business. Your marketing team should be clear about the most effective way to nurture those leads to determine whether those potential clients are the right fit for your business. Your relationship managers should be clear about the timeline the potential client wishes to engage in and what value that potential client sees in the wealth management services your firm offers. Your relationship

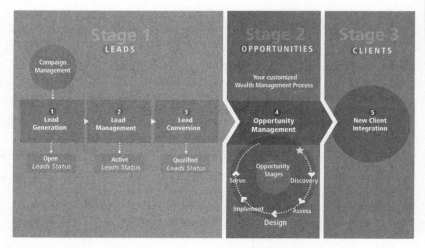

Figure 9.3 The Three Stages of the Client Acquisition Process™

managers should also set expectations before your team partners with the client so that clear outcomes are outlined and an appropriate timeline—one that works for both client and firm—to achieve those outcomes is established.

I find it important at this point to make the following recommendations. Often the teams' timeline is faster than that of the potential client. Therefore, let the client know that to deliver on the promises you're making, you'll need to marshal the resources to get it right. You'll need to know what his or her timeline looks like, so you can best move at the pace at which he or she wishes to move. This demonstrates your sincere desire to honor their timeline while also allowing you and your team to deliver.

Also, it's important at this stage to be absolutely certain that you get a commitment from the prospective client that, no matter what, lines of communication will remain open. No one ever likes a prospect that goes dark. By setting the stage and agreement up front that this won't be the case, if and when it does, you'll have a terrific way to go back to the client and remind the client of your agreement or you'll decide that this prospective client and his or her communication style are just not the right fit for your business.

Once you determine that a lead is either interested in working with your firm or qualified to work with your firm, you move into Stage 2,

Opportunity Management. Your lead is now an opportunity because he or she has shown interest or shown evidence of being qualified to work with you, increasing the chances that he or she will ultimately convert to being your client.

In Stage 2, it is time to go deeper in helping prospective clients understand your frame by allowing them to take your firm for a "test drive." Introduce them to your team, take time to explain your customized wealth management processes, and perhaps even offer them, in vivo, a sampling of what you do so they can get a feel for its value firsthand. This may entail sharing some of your unique materials, such as checklists, white papers, or self-assessments, or it might involve going so far as to create a financial plan together. During Stage 2, you will use your customized wealth management process to engage the prospective client and provide an opportunity for him or her to sample the value of your firm's signature approach.

Ultimately, you will design Stage 2 in a way that works best for your firm, but the following five steps can offer you a generic starting point:

1. *Discover* everything you can learn about the prospective client.
2. *Assess* the prospective client's current situation.
3. *Design* a wealth plan in complete partnership with the prospective client.
4. *Introduce* the wealth plan and begin the process of delivering value.
5. *Invite* the prospective client to sign on as a client with your firm so that you may implement the wealth plan and start serving the client in a complete wealth management way.

These five steps represent a generic approach to Stage 2, and we recognize that many advisors will want to customize it to meet their business and client needs. If you have not already, we encourage you to customize your process, both for your comfort and to individualize your approach to the specific clients you are working with. These five steps can provide a starting point.

By learning more about the prospective client and allowing him or her to learn more about your firm, you can use Stage 2 to determine whether the prospective client is both interested *and* qualified to work with your firm. If the client emerges as being both, ask him or her to become a client. Enter Stage 3: New Client Integration.

Stage 3 begins once a prospective client has agreed to work with your firm. It's time for onboarding. Regardless of how effective your firm was at conducting Stages 1 and 2, this next stage of onboarding is equally essential to the process to ensure the longevity of the client relationship. Successful onboarding can be achieved by delivering to the client the value that was promised to him or her during Stages 1 and 2.

During Stage 3, you will welcome your new client and deepen the relationship; you will get the appropriate paperwork completed and begin all of the technical work required to set up a new client within the firm. You may share guidelines for what is expected for how you work with clients and how they are invited to partner with the firm. Every firm has its own unique onboarding process; you can go to the ClientWise eXchange™ to get other ideas and tools to help you design your own process. First impressions last a lifetime, so plan to get it right up front!

KEY CONCEPT

The next step of your focused growth and change as a firm is acquiring new clients. This often happens quite naturally, as your deliberate crafting of services and clear vision of what you do attracts people who share your outlook and need your specific talents.

THE eXchange™
Online Tool 9.1: Ninety-Nine Discovery Questions

Much has been written about the discovery phase of wealth management, but if you would like additional support, feel free to visit the eXchange™ to access 99 discovery questions you can use in this first stage of the wealth management process.

At ClientWise, we've been tracking those advisors who have had extraordinary success for multiple years in a row, bringing in new clients, acquiring new relationships, and uncovering new client assets and opportunities to serve. Advisors are often asking me, because we coach so many top professionals, what's the secret to client acquisition? What are the best in the business doing to grow their client base? The answer is pretty simple, but very few execute on this. First, the best in the business are clear about how they want to be framed and intentional about being consistent. They are selective. They don't take every client. They turn away from opportunities where they wouldn't be at their best and help those they turn away find the appropriate financial professional. In other words, they know who they serve and they're focused! Second, they have built a process. Oftentimes, they follow our proven process for Building Loyal Client Advocates™ and are intentional about building their Professional Advocate Network™. Yes, it's true. They look for introductions, not referrals. Loyal client advocates and professional advocates accont for more than 70 percent of net new relationships among those who are having extraordinary success bringing on new relationships.

THE eXchange™
Online Tool 9.2: Improve Your Client Acquisition Process

For a printable copy of the Three Stages of the Client Acquisition Process™, along with an associated exercise to help you improve your current process and set goals, visit the eXchange™.

CONCLUSION

At its core, step 4, renewing relationships, is about engaging in a conversation with clients who have known you all these years so you can reframe yourself and your firm for them. Knowingly or unknowingly, you've trained your clients over time to see you in a certain way; now it's time to retrain them to understand the new and improved value you provide for the fee that you are charging them.

Of course, this is much more than an opportunity to teach clients about your new frame and your new and improved value to them as a firm. It's an essential moment to deepen your relationship with the clients—both their trust in you and their belief that you are the right firm for them.

You go into the Client Renewal Conversation with a client-centered attitude that the client can detect and appreciate. You inform the client of the ways in which you heard what was said in that earlier ClientWise Conversation™, along with the feedback of other clients, and demonstrate how you have decided to incorporate that feedback into your new frame.

Learning can become wisdom when you understand it consciously and can share it with someone else. Renewing relationships is an opportunity to turn the learning you've experienced during earlier stages of the reframe into just such wisdom.

With your existing client relationships renewed and your frame well defined and designed, you are ready to carry the frame into the future. This will involve teaching new clients about your frame as you acquire and integrate them into your practice. It also should involve generating ongoing content that allows you to continue educating your clients to understand and value your new frame: blog posts, white papers, e-newsletters, freebie checklists, assessments, and whatever other materials you have cited as candidates for your marketing campaign.

Remember: Whether you are courting prospective clients at an in-person meeting, generating ongoing marketing content, or meeting with an existing client for a review, it is ever so important to communicate your new frame in a consistent way. If you want people to think of you differently, you have to remain faithful to the message that you want to deliver each and every time you encounter them. It takes time for the message to settle in—and it's a good message that you've worked hard to craft. Capitalize on it!

NOTES

1. Kelly Campbell, personal interview, March 12, 2015, transcript, p. 4.
2. Ibid., p. 5.

CHAPTER **10**

Sharing the Frame
It's All About Advocacy

Your new frame would not be complete without a strong network of trusted professionals and clients to help you spread the word about the rich kind of wealth management you now deliver. At ClientWise, we call this network the *loyal advocate network* and consider it an essential part of any financial advisor's success. It is step 5 of the reframing process (see Figure 10.1). Here's why.

In ClientWise's research of more than 500 top financial advisors, advisors indicated that 71 percent of the business that they were currently winning was a direct result of new client relationships that had originated from introductions and personal connections through their network of advocates. In addition, our research showed that the most successful financial advisors spent 41 percent or more of their

Figure 10.1 Reframe Step 5: Create a Loyal Advocate Network

time in client outreach and acquisition, and that the method for client acquisition with the most effective results, in terms of assets collected, was an advocate approach.

At ClientWise, we feel that a robust advocate network is essential to the health and success of your business, which is why it is included as the fifth and last step of the reframing process. According to a study by the IBM Institute of Business Value,[1] other benefits of having a strong network of advocates include (1) advocates are 60 percent less likely to be sensitive to fees, and (2) advocates are twice as likely to consolidate 80 percent of their assets with one wealth management firm. At ClientWise, we have witnessed that advocates not only know the value of their advisors but are also glad to communicate it to others. Advocates are more than clients or professionals with whom you will engage; they are partners who will work with you toward a successful future.

 KEY CONCEPT

In a study of 500 financial advisors, nearly three-quarters of new business was found to have resulted from introductions and personal connections through an advocate network.

WHAT IS A LOYAL ADVOCATE?

Among the many words used to describe *advocate* are *backer, campaigner, champion, expounder, promoter, proponent, supporter,* and *upholder.*[2] According to Merriam-Webster,[3] an advocate is someone who "works for a cause or a group" or "a person who argues for or supports a cause or policy." In the context of growing your business, *advocate* has an even more particular meaning. At ClientWise, we don't just refer to advocates but to loyal advocates, and we define the term as follows.

A *loyal advocate* is someone who appreciates and understands what you do, thoroughly understands the benefits to themselves and others of being in a relationship with you, can clearly articulate both what you do and the benefits of it to others, and is actively engaged in introducing you to prospective clients for the benefit of you and the prospective client.

At the core of it, loyal advocates are *partners* with you, and you are partners with them. Worthy partners are those who believe and understand the value of the excellence and commitment that they bring to clients. Partners communicate, support one another, and are willing to help one another, oftentimes when there is no remuneration, because partners are playing the long game and they believe in the nobility of the work they are doing.

There are two kinds of loyal advocates:

- client advocates
- professional advocates.

The first group, Loyal Client Advocates™ (LCAs), consists of your clients who are willing to advocate for you. Many LCAs have such strong relationships with their financial advisors that they think and behave more like a partner than a client. Think about how powerful that is—to have your clients as partners. These are the clients who want to see you succeed; who will go out of their way to help you connect with those they believe will benefit from all that you offer; and who know that their friends, family, colleagues, and network are best served when they are working with you.

The second group consists of the professionals (e.g., business valuation specialists, business brokers, estate attorneys, CPAs, bankers, realtors, executive coaches, and physicians, just to name a few) who are willing to advocate for you and who seek to serve any mutual clients at a deeper level by being in a relationship with you. In truth, any professional who is on your external team should be a loyal advocate. If they are not, reconsider whether they should really be part of the team. Why would you send business to one of these other professionals on your wealth management team unless you could feel confident that they would advocate for you to their clients as well?

Both client and professional advocates meet a list of *seven specific criteria*. Loyal advocates

1. appreciate and understand what you do.
2. thoroughly understand the benefits of being in relationship with you.
3. are able to articulate well what you do and the benefits to others in a manner that is consistent with how you wish to be framed.
4. want to be actively engaged in partnering with you to make the necessary introductions to prospective clients for your benefit.
5. are natural connectors.
6. have influence with others when they make an introduction.
7. have a strong network of individuals to whom they can make useful introductions.

Let's look at each of those criteria more closely. It's a must that individuals be able to appreciate and understand you if they are to be loyal advocates. They also need to be able to articulate well what it is that you do. If they don't, they will just keep framing you to others using your old frame or will otherwise mis-frame you.

 KEY CONCEPT

Loyal advocates meet seven criteria: They understand what you do, understand the benefits of partnering with you, can communicate the benefits of partnering with you, can make introductions to prospective clients, are natural connectors, influence others, and have a strong network of individuals to introduce you to.

Beyond having the appreciation and ability to tell others accurately about what you do, individuals who are going to be your advocates need to be *connectors* and *influencers*: those who find it easy to connect you to others and enjoy making introductions (connectors) and who are also able to impact the decisions that these people make because they are held in high esteem by them (influencers).

Connectors and influencers are more than people who have a network; they are people who are able to effectively use their network or "Rolodex." Knowing how to take that Rolodex and introduce others to your network is what connecting is all about. After those introductions are made, influence is the invaluable quality of having the standing that allows a person to influence people. Also important, loyal advocates can make qualified connections—that is, introduce you to people that matter to you and your business.

I know lots of people who have a network but don't know how to make an introduction, and, when they do, it doesn't come with ease. I also know lots of folks who both have a network and are able, with ease, to make a connection, but they have no influence, so when they make an introduction, it generally falls flat because the person who is being introduced is bothered by the introduction. "Oh goodness, why again did you say Joe wants us to meet? He's always doing this and wasting my time!" Well, that won't go well. Get my point? You've got to build advocate relationships with those who meet all of these seven criteria, as each is an important part of enabling a valuable partnership.

Last, for individuals to become part of your loyal advocate network, they must have a willingness and capability to play the role of advocate for you. Ultimately, individuals can appreciate you and understand what you do, articulate well what you do, be a great connector, have influence, and know the right people, but if they don't want to be actively engaged in advocating for you, then they're not going to be able to help you gain the potential benefits of a loyal advocate network. They have to be motivated and willing to engage in the process.

KEY CONCEPT

The best loyal advocates are connectors, who have many contacts, and influencers, whose advice carries weight with the members of their network.

It's a lot to expect of people to be advocates. Is this realistic? Attainable? Results from an IBM Institute of Business study point in the direction of *yes*. Of 1,311 U.S. wealth management clients who had been with their firm for an average of 10+ years and who had investable assets over $500,000, 43 percent of these individuals identified themselves with characteristics of an advocate as defined in that study.[4] That is, they were likely to refer new business, consolidate more of their portfolios with their primary firm, and resist competitive offers.

Clearly, not every client will have the characteristics of an LCA as defined here in this chapter. In fact, most clients will not have all of the characteristics to be called an LCA. Given that reality, the top financial advisors focus on that small population of clients (5 percent or less) who want to be engaged with the financial advisor and who are most likely to provide new client introductions consistently and proactively. Not everyone has a network, nor the influence. Some are more comfortable than others in making an introduction. And others may not have the time to make an introduction. This is about quality over quantity.

If you are wondering how many advocates it is realistic to expect to attain, consider the following. It is reasonable to expect that each advisor on the team can attain five LCAs on his or her own. Generally, the leader or partners in the financial advisory firm or team take the role of developing professional advocates and strategic alliances. That being said, since these professional advocates are instrumental to delivering the promises made regarding wealth management, often it's the other advisors on the team that serve as the hands-on collaborators with the professionals for the benefit of the client.

Take a moment now to consider your loyal advocates. Who are they, and how do you know that they are able to advocate for you? Chances are that you've got some folks who are in the ballpark of being your advocates, but if they don't meet all seven criteria, they don't represent a loyal advocate—at least, not yet.

Unfortunately, most advisors think they have a lot of people who are advocating for them, when the truth of the matter is that they have a lot of people who may like them without being able to serve as real advocates. At ClientWise, we suggest using a formal process for building your network of advocates so you can be sure that you have true loyal advocates on your side. We call this process the *advocate approach*.

Creating LCAs is more than a key strategy to building your firm's client base—it's essential. At ClientWise, we believe in the power of LCAs to such a degree that we have developed a series of training programs on the subject, along with 45 pages of supporting material. While the present chapter does not provide enough space to cover the subject of LCAs to its fullest depth, it will give an overview of the process of building LCAs to provide greater insight to get you started.

Although I realize that not every reader will be interested in working with a coaching or consulting firm to help them build their LCA network, I would be doing advisors a disservice if I did not encourage them to consider doing so. In reality, there are many mistakes that advisors tend to make when building the LCA network and many pitfalls to the process; thus, it is truly helpful to have support to ensure that things go well. Because building the LCA network, with its seven criteria, is a unique process that ClientWise has designed, we have lots of useful insight into the specific ways to avoid these mistakes and pitfalls. We've built a series of programs to help advisors build their LCA network, whether they've got a week or 12 weeks and whether they are building LCAs on their own or embarking on a journey with their team. When you are ready to build your LCA network, I encourage you to consider availing yourself of a resource such as one of these programs.

 COACHING CORNER

Take some time to answer the following questions. Write them down or discuss them with another person on your team.

1. Are there any concepts about developing a team of loyal advocates that you are uncomfortable with or any beliefs you have that might limit your ability to develop your advocate network? If so, what are they and how will you move past them?

2. Why do you refer people to other professionals, and what can you learn from that process that will help you create your strategies for developing your loyal advocate network?

3. What would you like to shift or change in your thinking or actions to be more powerful in developing your loyal advocate network?

THE eXchange™
Online Tool 10.1: The Advocate Approach Self-Assessment™

ClientWise has created a tool to help you determine how engaged in the advocate approach you already are. The Advocate Approach Self-Assessment™ was developed to help you assess the depth and strength of your advocate approach in an easy and effective way. You can take the assessment by visiting the eXchange.™

 The Difference between a Referral and Advocacy

When most advisors hear the word *advocacy,* they think of referrals, but there is a difference. A referral is a simple act that occurs when someone gives your name and contact info to someone else and suggests they contact you to learn more about your services. Another version is when someone gives you a person's contact information and tells you to call them. You might hear, "Call my buddy Rick. He could really benefit from what you do." Or, "Call my kids and get to know them better." Then when you ask if the client wants to be involved in the process, he or she says no.

Advocacy, in contrast, occurs when a person is able to tell others about your services and is willing to take the time to make an introduction between you and the person. Whereas a referral involves just giving your contact info to someone else and leaving it to the person to possibly follow up, an introduction involves a person getting actively involved in connecting you with the prospective client. This could entail the advocate

- sending a joint e-mail to you and the person to get you connected,
- getting you both on the phone line together,
- or even arranging an in-person meeting with everyone present.

An advocate engages in a formal handoff between you and the client and then stays in touch to hear how things are going between the two of you. In fact, as you build your loyal advocates, both clients and professionals, you'll learn that the true advocate is eager to partner with you to determine together how a proper handoff should occur.

If you can't find yourself advocates, then a referral is better than nothing at all. And yet why not go deeper than a referral? An advocate offers so much more. First, people tend to be more inclined to follow up with you if you have been introduced to them by someone they know and respect, if only out of courtesy for their contact. Second, people tend to be more comfortable initiating a working relationship with those that are known by someone they know. A study by Nielsen gives some insight here: Ninety-two percent of global consumers report that they trust "earned media," such as word-of-mouth or recommendations from friends and family, above all other forms of advertising.[5]

Third, advocates—true loyal advocates who meet the seven criteria—can be relied upon to generate new business for you more effectively than referrals. They are not only willing to be actively involved in helping you grow your business, but they also have the contacts, influence, and understanding of your business and its benefits to be able to do so.

It's always better for someone else to tell your story. Touting your own virtues can come across as sales-y; the listener knows at minimum that you are biased and have a vested interest in influencing them. In contrast, if a respected outside party is communicating your virtues to someone, the listener typically perceives more objectivity and credibility behind the positive words. Thus, the value of advocacy over referrals!

BUILDING CLIENT ADVOCATES

Most advisors know people who are willing to tell others about them and who are already doing so to the best of their ability. Yet, most people with the opportunity to advocate have difficulty transferring the trusting relationship they have with their advisor into a form of communication that really excites the potential new client.

The communication sometimes goes like this: "You have to meet my advisor. I have the best relationship with [him/her]." Or "She's a great money manager." Or "He's really good at helping you choose the right insurance plan." Unfortunately, the family member, friend, or colleague hearing these words does not necessarily discover the value for him- or herself in generic statements like these. The advocate approach can be used to enable advisors to help others describe what these advisors do in a way that's unique, differentiating, and compelling to potential clients.

Benefits of the Advocate Approach

The advocate approach was developed in response to research that ClientWise conducted with over 500 of the most successful financial advisors in the business who have vibrant, highly profitable practices. This approach was then field-tested. For those financial advisors who followed the steps of the advocate approach and did the necessary work, the approach created highly successful results with significant growth in client numbers, amount of assets managed, and significant increases in revenue for the financial advisor. To see the potential that engaging in this process holds for you, conduct the exercise in Figure 10.2.

Enter your best estimates in the fields of Figure 10.2 and do the calculations to get a clearer idea of what the payoff could be in building an LCA network for your firm.

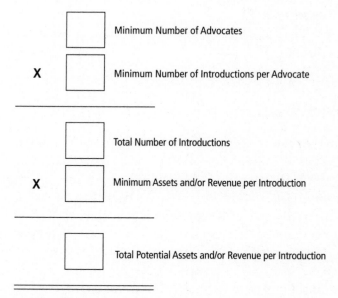

Figure 10.2 Total Potential Value of the LCA Network

This exercise allows you to put into real numbers the benefits of using the advocate approach. For example, if a financial advisor cultivated only a small contingent of three to five client advocates who, in turn, introduced three to five of their close associates, friends, and family throughout the course of the year, that would lead to 10 to 25 new client relationships annually for your business. In turn, if the same numbers applied when building professional advocates, that number would double, leading to a total of 20 to 50 new client relationships each year. That's more than power in numbers—it's power in relationships. Over the last decade in coaching advisors and teams building these processes, I've learned firsthand that the advocate is the gift that keeps on giving. Once you establish the advocate partnership and nurture the relationship by building a custom service model for them, they not only will continue to share their relationships and network with you, they will also accelerate the sharing. You'll find you have more and more in common over the many years you'll work intentionally together. One key hint here: You must build a custom service model for them and continue to spend time together. This is step 5 of the process, and you'll hear more about this later in this chapter.

KEY CONCEPT

Using the advocate approach can grow your business exponentially. Do not underestimate its importance.

The advocacy approach has five steps, as shown in Figure 10.3. It's an elegant process, one that should be learned and mastered by all of the members of your team, especially your lead advisors.

Discover

The advocate approach begins with something you already know well: having the ClientWise Conversation™ with a client. The goal here

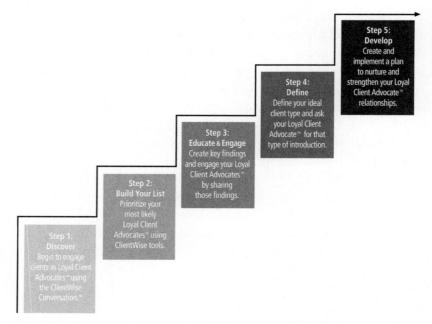

Figure 10.3 Five Steps to Building Loyal Client Advocates™

is to get a sense of whether the client appreciates and understands what you do, understands the benefits received by being in a relationship with you, and can articulate them. Here, you are *discovering*, or assessing, whether this particular client is well suited to be an advocate for you. In addition, you are gathering information on any other professionals that you may want to bring into your advocate network.

It's now time to pick up the phone and ask your most promising potential advocates for a face-to-face meeting. Your side of the conversation doesn't have to follow this script exactly, but the gist will be this: "As my business continues to grow, I'm always looking for ways to improve what it is that we do as a firm to serve clients just like you. I'm meeting with a very select group; I value your opinion and would welcome your feedback on a few items. Would you be willing to meet with me for twenty to thirty minutes over a cup of coffee or lunch?"

When you meet with your client, begin the ClientWise Conversation™. Let's review the five questions that make up the ClientWise Conversation™:

1. What is the one thing you value most about how my firm and I serve you?
2. What is the one thing you would most like me to change or improve about my firm and how I serve you?
3. If you were to describe the services that my firm and I offer you, to clients like yourself, what would you say?
4. If you were to describe what we've achieved together for as long as we've worked together, what would you say?
5. Among your other professional advisors in your life, who do you trust the most and why?

By the time clients are done answering these questions, you will have a clearer sense of how well they understand and appreciate what you do, as well as how effective they are at articulating your frame. You also will receive a review of their trusted advisors, or even possibly get the names of some new ones for you to reach out to.

You will need to think about how and when to reintroduce the ClientWise Conversation.™ You've already conducted it once, but this will be your chance to do so again, since your client has been informed about your new frame.

As for when, let some time pass between when you conducted your last conversation with the client (which will be the Client Renewal Conversation) and when you conduct the next ClientWise Conversation™ to be respectful of the client's time. This will also give the client the opportunity to experience receiving your services and support within your new frame, before you jump back in to learn more about how well they understand and appreciate what you do and how well they can articulate what you offer. Leave this up to the client, but there will be some that you go back to and some you won't. For the ones you do return to, you shouldn't wait more than six to eight weeks at the most.

Some advisors worry about bothering the client with another conversation. That is why we are careful to allow sufficient time to pass between the Client Renewal Conversation and the next ClientWise Conversation™. In addition, the ClientWise Conversation™, with its very specific steps and recommendations around how to conduct it, will ensure that you remain respectful of the client when speaking to him or her (see Chapter 6 for details). Remember, too, that it is recommended that you conduct the ClientWise Conversation™ on a periodic basis with every client to gauge from time to time how effectively you are framing your firm. You are not conducting this conversation for self-serving reasons but because you truly want to serve the clients better by understanding from their answers how you are doing in their eyes.

KEY CONCEPT

The first step of the advocate approach is discovery, which is accomplished through a face-to-face meeting and ClientWise Conversation™ with the client. Discuss what and how your firm is doing and assess whether the client can articulate your new frame accurately to potential new clients.

As you proceed through the ClientWise Conversation™ with your clients, we recommend that you begin to segment your clients into those who are already LCAs, those who have the potential to be LCAs, and those who are not likely to be loyal advocates.

THE eXchange™
Online Tool 10.2: Potential Client Advocate Checklist

Visit the eXchange™ for a checklist that will help you categorize clients as loyal advocates versus potential loyal advocates.

Build Your List

After you conduct the ClientWise Conversation™, it's time to build your list of potential client advocates (professional advocates come later in the process). To make that determination, you will have to consider which clients are currently actively engaged in partnering with you to make the necessary introductions to prospective clients for your benefit and the benefit of the prospective client. Evaluate who is sending you new clients, at what level are they sending you new clients, how valuable those introductions are, and whether the number of introductions from each client is increasing or decreasing. From there, you will be able to determine and build a list of which of your clients will be your best LCAs.

It bears repeating that not all clients will become (or have the potential to become) client advocates. In truth, you will have more clients who are not client advocates than those who are. As a result, you will want to invest your time in developing advocacy with those clients who either are already or are likely to become an integral part of your advocate network.

 KEY CONCEPT

After discovering your clients' potential as advocates through ClientWise Conversations™, consider how many new clients your current clients have already sent your way. With this information in hand, build a list of clients who show the most promise of being LCAs.

As you determine who your current LCAs are, consider the following points as well. Those clients with the potential to be loyal advocates generally provide multiple introductions, and established advocates almost always generate multiple introductions. In addition, advocates enjoy sending good, valuable introductions to you, not just individuals who have little potential to serve your practice. Indeed, some advocates refer clients who generate fees that are worth as much, if not more, than the original referring source. Plan to track where your introductions to new clients are coming from so you can be sure to get clear on who your strongest LCAs are.

THE eXchange™

Online Tool 10.3: New Client Introduction Tracking Sheet

Visit the eXchange™ to download a New Client Introduction Tracking Sheet that you can use while assessing your introductions over the past 24 months. You can also use this tracking sheet going forward to keep a record of every new introduction.

COACHING CORNER

Take time to sit down and look at your introductions for the last 24 months by clients. List which clients have sent you new clients and their level of assets.

Educate and Engage

After you have interviewed your clients with the ClientWise Conversation™ and built your list of current and potential LCAs, you are ready to assess the findings of the recent ClientWise Conversation™ and share those findings with the clients.

THE eXchange™

Online Tool 10.4: Loyal Client Advocate Approach™ Key Findings Worksheet

Go to the eXchange™ and download the Loyal Client Advocate Approach™ Key Findings Worksheet for help summarizing key data you gathered during the ClientWise Conversation™.

Once you have a handle on the findings of the ClientWise Conversation™, approach your current and potential client advocates on the phone to educate and engage them. Take this time to share the ClientWise Conversation™ findings with these clients and ask to set up a meeting to discuss the clients' advocacy or possible advocacy.

As a review of the steps just discussed and to expand on them, the process should go as follows:

- Request a meeting by phone.
- State the purpose of the meeting (to share what you've learned from the ClientWise Conversation™ and get the client's take on whether he or she thinks you've gotten it right, or not).
- Share the key findings from your worksheet.
- Acknowledge the client's continued help and insights, and mention two or three things that have been useful from the conversation. It is important that you offer things that have been authentically useful or illuminating for you.
- Ask the client for permission to have a third, larger conversation.

Note that you will not have this educate-and-engage conversation with all of the clients who you initially interviewed at the beginning of the advocacy approach. You will use the results from the Loyal Client Advocate Approach™ Key Findings Worksheet—and your intuition and discretion—to determine how many clients you intend to educate and engage and who those clients are. Plan to start with those clients who already appear to be advocates and then move to those who appear to be potential advocates. Prioritize who you speak with first on the basis of where you see the best potential for return on your time and effort and the best potential to build deeper, more engaged relationships.

Note that there will be some clients that you will determine, based on their feedback, that you're not likely to return to. However, those that were eager to connect with you and were willing to share their input, you will likely want to go back to. These are the folks that will be eager to learn what you've discovered and who want to know about the changes and improvements you plan on making to your business and team.

When you request another meeting, be sure to protect the relationship by giving the client permission to say no if the client appears hesitant. At this point, the client will have either said an unqualified yes, maybe, or no. Don't push for a yes if the client is reluctant. You will have a chance to ask again if you think that it will not injure the relationship. If the client says no, accept it gracefully and thank the client again for his or her time and opinions to date. For those clients who are willing to have the next meeting, thank them and tell them you will call in the next week or so to schedule another conversation. That conversation will be step 4, define, in the Loyal Client Advocate Approach™.

Finally, watch your time. This conversation should last no more than an hour unless the client seems to be so engaged that he or she doesn't want to stop. It is critically important that in that hour, you complete the entire conversation.

 KEY CONCEPT

The next step of building LCAs is educating and engaging the clients you have identified as potential advocates. Via phone call, share what you've learned in past conversations, acknowledge their past help and insights, and ask for a third in-person conversation to explore their future advocacy. If your client seems reluctant to step into the advocate role, do not push.

Define

You have now laid the foundation for conversation. You have done the research, identified your highest potential LCAs, and asked them for a larger conversation about working more closely with you. You have a list of clients who have indicated that they are willing and want to have this larger conversation with you. You are now ready for the conversation that actually moves into your most important request of your LCAs: the request for introductions.

What you will be engaging in is not the typical referral conversation; this part of the conversation will help you create a working relationship with your client. It will teach you how to ask for the right kind of introduction so that your client can connect you to exactly the kind of prospective clients you are looking for: the ideal client that you defined when creating your new frame.

The conversation will be as follows:

- Request a meeting by phone.
- State the purpose of the meeting at its beginning.

- Protect the relationship by providing an out if the client is not willing to become engaged on a deeper level with you and your practice.
- Protect the relationship by reinforcing confidentiality.
- Ask directly for the client to work closer with you to develop new clients.
- Share your ideal client type.
- Be specific in asking the client to make an introduction.
- Thank the LCA for the conversation and any introductions that have been given, and ask whether you can be of service in any way to the LCA.

For those who are potential advocates, you will aim to educate and engage them around advocacy; for those who are already your advocates, you can focus on deepening their connection to their role as an advocate.

KEY CONCEPT

The next step of the advocate approach is to meet again with your potential advocate in person. Ask the client to work closely with you to develop new clients for your firm, but be aware of any hesitance on your client's part; protect your relationship and reinforce confidentiality with your client before all other considerations. Identify your ideal client type, specifically ask for introductions, sincerely thank your LCA, and ask how you can be of service to the LCA.

A Conversation Script: Inviting Clients to Be Loyal Advocates

1. **Request a meeting by phone.**

   Hello, Karen. In our last meeting, I mentioned I would like to have a larger conversation with you and you were generously willing to do that. I am looking forward to that conversation

   (Continued)

(*Continued*)

and wanted to get it on the calendar. Would you be available to meet with me in the next few days or next week?

2. **State the purpose of the meeting at its beginning.**

    When we last met, I said that I wanted to have a larger conversation about working closer with you in growing my business selectively. I want to share my vision around that, get your input, and ask for your help.

3. **Protect the relationship by providing an out if the client is not willing to become engaged on a deeper level with you and your practice.**

    As I stated last time, I want you to know that our friendship comes first. Whatever else may happen, it is critically important to me that we protect our relationship. So, please feel free to let me know if at any time I have asked something that doesn't feel right for you.

4. **Protect the relationship by reinforcing confidentiality.**

    It goes without saying, but I'd like to say it anyway. Confidentiality is key. I view all of my conversations with all of my clients with the highest degree of confidentiality. You can be assured that I will never betray that sense of trust and privacy.

5. **Ask directly for the client to work closer with you to develop new clients**.

    Karen, would you be willing to be in a working relationship with me to help me find individuals like you who need and would benefit from the wealth management services that I provide?

6. **Share your ideal client type**.

    Karen, I really appreciate your partnership. As you think about those who might benefit from my services, I want you to know that experience has shown me that I am most effective serving the following types of clients. [You would then go on to explain your ideal client type or types, leaving room for your potential LCA to ask questions, make suggestions, or put forth the name of a potential client.]

7. **Be specific in asking the client to make an introduction.**

    Once you have explained your ideal client type, ask your LCA for introductions of that type. In addition, if you know the name of someone the LCA could introduce you to, ask for an introduction to that person, specifically using language similar to the language below.

    Karen, in the past you've spoken about Hal Holcrumb. As you mentioned, I focus on working with executives at manufacturing firms. I'd like to ask you a question. Knowing what you know about me and how I like to serve and work with clients like you, do you think that Mr. Holcrumb is the sort of person who I'd like to work with?

8. **Thank the LCA for the conversation, any introductions that have been made, and ask whether you can be of service in any way to the LCA.**

    Because you are building a deeper relationship with the LCA, it is critical that every conversation end with a personal acknowledgment of and thanks to the LCA. In addition, since the LCA is supporting you at a significant level, it is important that you seek to support the LCA in the same manner. I discuss that more fully in the next section.

Develop

You now have active LCAs. You have done the work to start the relationships and are on your way to finding these relationships rewarding both personally and professionally. Indeed, most financial advisors who develop LCAs regard them as some of the most meaningful and significant relationships in their lives.

Those financial advisors have not only undertaken the actions that create the relationships, they have also continued to *nurture and deepen* their LCA relationships. They do this not only because it makes sense from a business standpoint but also because the relationships create a foundational community of good, successful people who support one another.

Your work moving forward will be to design how you will develop, nurture, and sustain your LCA community. You must start by recognizing that the LCA relationship is different from your relationships with other clients. The client advocate relationship, at its best, is a tremendously intimate relationship because LCAs regularly put their reputations at risk by recommending you. They have that much faith in who you are and that much faith in your ability to serve those who are important to them.

You must recognize the scope of the LCA's very personal investment in a working relationship with you in your business and engage with him or her with equal personal investment. To nurture and sustain these relationships, you must do three things:

1. Develop rules and a structure for handling introductions with each LCA into which the LCA has real input.
2. Develop a special service model for LCAs that reflects the depth of your relationship with your LCAs.
3. Stay in touch with your LCAs regularly and at a significant level.

None of these actions are particularly difficult to achieve, but they all take intention, partnership with your LCAs, and a personal touch on your part. Much has been written about the best, most effective ways to generate referrals, but note that this method is not about generating an endless stream of referrals. Rather, it is about partnering with a select group of clients who meet all of the criteria to be considered advocates.

 KEY CONCEPT

Now that you have LCAs, take care of them. Take every opportunity to nurture and deepen your partnering relationship. They are putting their reputations on the line by recommending you and your services. Stay in touch and truly listen to what they have to say.

BUILDING PROFESSIONAL ADVOCATES

In addition to client advocates, professional advocates represent the other side of the advocacy coin that is so important to developing a successful wealth management practice, and the last important piece of the reframing process. Professional advocates are important in part because they will provide you with introductions to new clients, but also because you will need them to support your clients and wealth management business; thus, you will want to introduce your clients to these professionals as well. At ClientWise, what we've learned is that the best in the business are building these networks of other professionals, not only for business development opportunities, but more so because to fulfill the promises made to clients, they will need a team of other professionals to round out their own wealth management business. The quality introductions from these other professionals should only be considered a strategic by-product of building the network correctly.

For example, most advisors will not be involved in doing a client's taxes, preparing their estate documents, valuing their business for sale, providing a client's life insurance solutions, and so forth. As a result, working closely with other professionals who can provide these services becomes paramount. Advisors need other professionals in their network both to win new business and to support their clients in the best way possible.

The process of building professional advocates is similar to (although not the same as) the process of building client advocates. While the remainder of this chapter will not delve in depth into the how-to's of building professional advocates, Figure 10.4 provides an overview of the process that you can review to gain greater insight.

To build a professional advocate program with the greatest growth potential possible, we recommend that you seek the help of a coach or mentor for each step. To help you implement the tools in this program rapidly and in a fully customized way, you may wish to seek the help of a professional coach who has a complete coaching skill set as well as experience in the industry. ClientWise also offers in-depth training on this topic, which goes beyond what could realistically be included in this chapter.

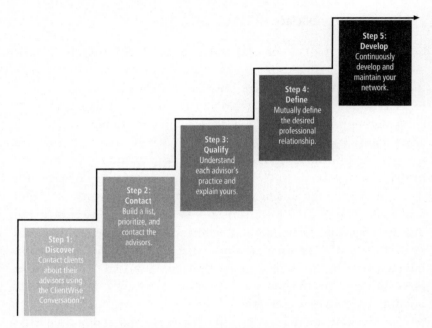

Figure 10.4 Five Steps to Building Professional Advocates

Steps 1 and 2: Discover and Contact

You have already conducted the first step of this process when building your LCAs, so you will not need to repeat that step now, but it is included here to show the full process from start to finish.

The second step is to build your list of potential professional advocates, to categorize and prioritize them according to current versus potential advocates, and then to contact these professionals. When deciding who goes on this list, don't just include the professionals that your clients recommended—also consider all of the professionals you already know and/or work with. Aim for a list of 50 to 75 professionals and centers of influence.

There are many centers of influence to consider as your advocates. For some on this list, the introduction process will be a two-way street; for others, it is just a one-way boulevard in your direction.

- Valuation consultant or business broker
- Realtor

- Certified public accountant
- Personal coach or advisor
- Attorney
- Chamber of Commerce leader
- Business owner
- Community or political leader
- Other financial advisors
- Doctor
- Church or synagogue leader
- Professor, teacher, principal, other school officials

This list of possible centers of influence can help you brainstorm who you'd like to include on your customized list of potential professional advocates.

After collecting the names and phone numbers of other professional advisors and centers of influence from your clients, it is time to list and prioritize them. To ensure that you are investing your resources where they are most likely to pay off, it is helpful to focus first on those professional advisors who will help you best serve your ideal client type, as defined by you during the earlier step 2 of the reframing process (see Figure 10.5).

Once your list of professionals is built, it's time to contact your target professionals. One of the hardest things for some financial professionals is to make the first contact with another advisor. Even though it may be uncomfortable, your goal should be to meet with every one of the high-potential professionals mentioned to you during your client meetings.

Figure 10.5 Priority Categories for Potential Professional Advocates

Will everyone respond positively to your request and be willing to meet with you? No. But a surprising percentage of professionals will, and many of the most successful centers of influence in your community will be happy to, as well. The most successful financial advisors have learned that their success is directly related to their degree of connectedness to others in the community. On the basis of our research and experience at ClientWise, I can confidently predict that at least half of the people you call will meet with you.

KEY CONCEPT

Another source of advocates is your and your clients' professional networks. Follow similar steps (discover, contact, qualify, define, develop) to engage professional advocates as you do for client advocates, but look to people you work with, people your clients work with, and other centers of influence when considering who to recruit for your network.

COACHING CORNER

Take some time to think about centers of influence you know who could potentially be good advocates for you and your business.

Step 3: Qualify

The third step of building professional advocates is to understand each professional's practice and explain your practice as well to these advocates—to deliver your frame. We recommend that you do this in two separate meetings, using the first meeting to learn about what the professional does in his or her practice and then, if you are still interested in working with this professional, using the second meeting to educate the professional on your own frame.

At the first meeting, plan to

1. set the agenda (i.e., purpose of the meeting, what you want to cover, the amount of time allocated, and "check-in for acceptance");

2. ask specific questions to better understand the professional advisor and his or her practice, and take notes;

3. begin to discern whether you want to work with this professional advisor; and

4. schedule the next appointment, if you see the potential for a mutually beneficial relationship.

Some sample questions to consider asking are

- How did you get started in your profession?
- What is it about your profession that appeals most to you?
- What distinguishes you from others in your field?
- In your opinion, what is the most challenging factor people in your profession face today?
- How do you promote your services?
- With the exception of anything that might be considered confidential, what are some of the things you and our mutual client have accomplished?

After the interview is complete, take time to discern whether you want to work with this professional advisor. Follow the guidance of author Janet G. Elsea in her book *First Impression Best Impression* and consider what the professional looked like during the interview, what he or she sounded like, what he or she said, and how well he or she listened. What are your initial instincts, thoughts, and/or feelings regarding whether you would be able to have a productive relationship with this professional?

THE eXchange™

Online Tool 10.5: Interview Questions for Potential Professional Advocates

For a list of additional possible questions to ask potential professional advocates, visit the eXchange™.

At the second meeting with the professional with whom you'd like to collaborate, it's time to take out your capability deck and use it to communicate all that you now do. That's step 4 of the following recommended process:

1. Set the agenda (i.e., purpose of the meeting, what you want to cover, the amount of time allocated, and "check-in for acceptance").

2. Recap what you learned from the first meeting to confirm your understanding and convey that you listened carefully to what the professional advisor had to say. Look for an acknowledgment from the professional advisor that you got it right. Now you may move forward.

3. Once you've received that acknowledgment, ask for permission to discuss your practice.

4. Run the professional through your capability presentation to educate them on your frame.

5. Ask the professional advisor how he or she would describe you and your practice.

6. Schedule the next appointment to manage expectations and mutually define the desired introduction relationship, which is to be based on mutual advocacy.

▼ Advocates as a Sounding Board but Not an Advisory Council

As you are making decisions about how to change and improve your firm and how to grow your business, your advocates can be your sounding board to get direct feedback on your services, your offerings, and the decisions you need to make. This approach is not to be confused with creating an advisory council or an advisory board. While I've seen those work remarkably successfully, one of the things I would caution advisors against is creating an advisory board with a formal structure, because that often comes with unintended consequences.

The two most significant potential unintended consequences are as follows. First, some of your advocates may not get along with each other and may not want to serve on a board more formally together. Second, boards have term limits, and you want your advocates to be evergreen rather than having a term limit attached. Because of these unintended consequences, I'm not a fan of formalizing an advisory board. From time to time, though, it makes sense to pull advocates together as a sounding board.

Step 4: Define

Once the proper groundwork has been laid (as described in the previous three steps), it is time to talk business from a mutual advocacy perspective. The third meeting is when you mutually define the desired professional relationship. Start, as always, with you setting the agenda. Next, acknowledge what you value most about the other professional advisor's practice and then seek an acknowledgment about what he or she values most about your practice. You might also discuss the synergies in the way each of you serves your clients.

You can then proceed to ask the professional advisor to describe his or her most desired client types so you understand what type of introduction the advisor would most like you to make for him or her, followed by you describing your most desired client type.

Last, plan to discuss your expectations for the relationship with the other professional. Keep focused on the possibilities of working together and discuss what that might look like. Authenticity and openness are fundamental to establishing and maintaining productive relationships.

Once you and another professional advisor understand each other's most desired client types, it is important to promptly manage each other's expectations about how you might collaborate and work together for the benefit of others. Nothing strains a new advocacy relationship faster than one party thinking (often erroneously) that the other is not holding up their end of the bargain. It may be helpful to summarize your working relationship in a document or e-mail, so you both can use it for reference.

Step 5: Develop

The last step in the process of building your professional advocate network is to continuously develop and maintain the network you've worked so hard to initiate. Plan to speak and meet with your professional advocates on a regular basis, as often as monthly, if possible. Over time, if your relationship with a particular network member proves to be unproductive for you despite your best efforts, drop it and invest your resources where they are likely to produce a better return.

Remember, it's not quantity that counts here, but quality. You don't need to have a list of 50 professional advocates. No one has the time or resources to maintain that many relationships. A handful of professional advisors who are committed to working closely with you for mutually beneficial reasons is all you need.

CONCLUSION

Why advocacy? When it comes to informing potential clients about your services, it's always better to have somebody else tell your story than for you to. This applies as much to family members and heirs as it does to any other type of new client.

Isn't it better to have your clients advocate to their family for the work that you have done together than for you to just singlehandedly try to build relationships with their kids and grandkids and inheritors of the clients' wealth? Credibility is so much stronger this way. As a result, the most important work you can do as an advisor is to proactively, intentionally build relationships with others who will serve as your advocates and be able to tell your story, in some ways perhaps even more elegantly and authentically than you can.

Note that even if your current clients are already advocating for you to others—friends, colleagues, families, and so on—you've still got to check back in continually with clients to keep them up to date on your services because your firm is evolving and growing, too. So you've always got to be educating your advocates—always updating and inviting them to learn more about the changes and improvements that you're making and informing them how you're proactively building out your team and your firm to meet the ever-changing needs of the financial services environment because it's a moving target. You will know your advocacy approach is working well when you start to witness that you're getting new clients from your loyal advocates and when you observe that your loyal advocates see great value in the work that you do by the words they use to describe your services.

Sustainable growth gets easier over time when others are advocating for your services. There's a bonus, too: It always feels good when others go out of their way to help you succeed. It's humbling that your advocates believe in the greater good of what you, your team, and your firm are all about.

Transfer of trust is easier when an advocate makes that handoff.

NOTES

1. Brian Lincoln and Bob Heffernan, *Building Client Advocacy: New Opportunities for Wealth Management Firms*. IBM Institute for Business Value, 2008, www.ibm.com/services/us/gbs/bus/pdf/gbw03021-usen-02-advocacy-wm.pdf.

2. *Roget's New Millennium Thesaurus*, 1st ed. (version 1.2.1), s.v. "advocate."

3. *Merriam-Webster OnLine*, s.v. "advocate," accessed May 6, 2015, www.merriam-webster.com/dictionary/advocate.

4. Lincoln and Heffernan, *Building Client Advocacy*.

5. "Global Trust in Advertising and Brand Messages," Nielsen Company, last modified April 10, 2012, accessed May 6, 2015, www.nielsen.com/us/en/insights/reports/2012/global-trust-in-advertising-and-brand-messages.html.

Conclusion

Ten Signals of a Successful Reframe

You've made it to the end of this book and, if you've been working the program as you go, very possibly the end of the reframing process for yourself and your firm. The question now is, how will you know if your reframe has been successful?

Like smoke signals that are used to communicate from a long distance, there are also signals that will appear after you've engaged in the reframe process that will provide you with insight that you are making progress on your reframing journey. These are universal signals for which you can be on the lookout, regardless of your particular reframe.

Then, there will be those signals that are unique to your firm and its particular reframe. This chapter provides guidance on both types of signals, describing what the common signals of success are as well as how to develop a list of customized signals to help you know that your unique reframe is going well.

239

But first, let's talk about this notion of an end to the reframing process. While it is true that there are five clear steps to reframing your wealth management firm, the truth is that reframing is an ongoing journey. *It's about dialogue as much as it is about destination.* The process of reframing is really one big feedback loop between your firm and your clients that should continue over months and years. This dialogue between you and your clients (as well as between you and your network of advocates) will enable your firm to continue to evolve to meet the shifting needs of your clients as well as the changing demands of the financial landscape. A willingness to treat the reframing process as a continuing journey will enable you to not only grow with the times but also expand your career and practice in a way that satisfies you personally and professionally. In other words, what you've now learned is a sustainable process.

The reality is that there is no "shazam!" moment within the reframe process in which your business will be tidily wrapped up with a bow and done evolving. Your vision for your practice will change; you will receive input from clients and professionals that will help shape that change. There might be a need to introduce new services. Your logo might change. The tax code will get updated and you'll have to adjust to it. Your knowledge will grow and affect the way you run your practice. As a result, the reframe process will, by necessity, need to be continual rather than finite. As you continue to attract new talent to your business, their input will be valuable to co-creating your future firm.

And yet, as you work through any given reframe, you will arrive at clear vistas where you will be able to appreciate the growth you've engaged in and enjoy its benefits. From these vistas—solid plateaus to which you will ascend during your journey of reframing—you will discover that all of your strategizing, effort, and teamwork have culminated in something real and powerful. You will be able to assess your success on the basis of the unique milestones you have set for yourself, as well as the list in this chapter of 10 universal signals of success that occur with effective reframing. By becoming familiar with the universal and unique signals of success, you will have the information you need to recognize when your reframe process is going well and when it needs some adjusting.

KEY CONCEPT

Reframing is an ongoing journey, but there are milestones, both universal and unique, to look for to ascertain whether you have successfully reframed along the way.

YOU KNOW YOUR REFRAME IS WORKING IF . . .

By now, it is clear that the journey of reframing takes time, patience, and work. There may be times that you and your team will be slogging through the "foggy woods," unsure of the progress you've made and unclear just how close or far your destination really is. Keep the following in mind for just such a moment: *Do not quit,* because you might be closer than you think. Instead, keep your antennae up; look for clues that your reframe is working; and, when you discover them, notice, appreciate, and celebrate them.

After the reframe has begun, you will start to see things change; you will see flutters of progress, inertia that is transforming into movement. Be attuned to these initial signs of change because it is in these areas that you will discover the "juice" of motivation to keep you going; these initial signs also will give you the confidence to continue moving ahead with the reframe. Don't forget to take the time to look up, either—you may just see a smoke signal in the distance letting you know you are close.

Universal Signals That Your Reframe Is Working

The signals that your reframe is working track well to many of the aspects of the reframe that you've worked through, so they will likely sound familiar.

You will know that your reframe is working when:

- Your *team* works excitedly together to enact the frame you've mutually designed and you can see that team members feel they're partners in the delivery of the new frame.

- Your *clients* exhibit confidence in working with members of your team because they trust their technical capability, relational capability, decisional capability, problem-solving capability, and so on.

- You ask clients to describe what it is you have achieved in the number of years you've worked together and they have a powerful and valuable answer, one that reflects the very frame you intended to build.

- Each client review is more powerful than the last.

- Your business profits are rising and doubling every three to five years.

- Another professional invites you to join in serving one of his or her clients and that professional frames you in a way that's exactly as you want to be framed.

- You find that it has gotten easier to run your business because your team, your advocates, and your clients want you to succeed.

- You are attracting new young talent to your team each year with ease.

- You see loyalty and longevity in your existing employees, who are excited about the strategic plan for growth because they're equal partners in having created that plan.

- You've got an operating agreement and a mechanism in place for the other talented members of your firm to find their "path to partner" and potentially (or have already) become owners in a sustainable and growing business.

The universal signals of success are many, then, and these represent some of the top ones. There will be unique signals of success, too. Read on to learn more about detecting them.

KEY CONCEPT

Among the universal signals of a successful reframe are a loyal and engaged team; clients happy with your partnership and the results you achieve for them; rising profits; and goodwill and accurate framing from clients, partners, and employees.

THE eXchange™

Online Tool C.1: A Checklist: Signals of Reframing Success

Visit the eXchange™ for a downloadable checklist of these and other universal signals that your reframe has been a success.

Unique Signals That Your Reframe Is Working

In addition to the universal signals of success, you can gauge your progress against a list of signals that you've laid out for yourself in advance that are indicators of your success. Here are some tips on how to do so:

- Collaborate with your team members to develop a list of items that signal you are meeting with success. Be as specific as possible.
- Include project milestones on your list that will show you have accomplished a meaningful task or an initiative related to your reframe.
- Share this list with your advocates and invite their ideas, comments, and feedback.
- Update your list of unique signals on the basis of what you have learned from your advocates.
- Gather input from your loyal advocates and determine whether they also see a shift in the frame of your firm.

Once your list of unique signals has been completed, you can go about gathering information to help you see which signals are actually occurring.

KEY CONCEPT

Unique signals for gauging the success of your reframe can be whatever you feel represents what you want to achieve. Work with your team to figure out a list of milestones, share the list of milestones with advocates for feedback, update your list as necessary, and check back with your advocates to see if the milestones are being met and your frame is shifting per your plan.

It's critical that you do the following three things (which are the most effective) to gather this information: (1) make your own observations, (2) assess business results, and (3) invite feedback from clients and professionals. As for observations, watch your team in action, ask questions of your clients and listen to their answers, and check in with your advocates to get a sense of how things are going from an outside perspective.

Analyze business results by paying attention to important data such as how your client base is increasing, how many introductions you are receiving, for what percentage of clients you are serving additional family members, etc. Create metrics for analyzing your business that link to your strategic goals so you can truly assess how your business is growing.

Most important, return to your clients consistently and repeatedly to gain insight into how they think you are doing. What do they feel you have accomplished together? What do they value most about your services and support? Once you've gathered everyone's feedback and added it to your observations and the business results, you will be in a position to evaluate where you are as a firm and what, if anything, you still need to do to achieve a successful reframe.

KEY CONCEPT

Being aware of your firm's current situation is key for the evaluation process to be successful. Gather data and make observations, analyze your business results, and listen to client feedback to gauge your reframing success.

COACHING CORNER

Set aside 30 to 60 minutes to work with your team to identify what will constitute your unique signals of success. Plan to revisit that list with your team in a few months to assess which signals you have met so far; which you still hope to meet; which new signals you'd like to add; and which signals, if any, you feel missed the mark and should be removed from the list.

Ten Signals That Your Reframe *Isn't* Working

In spite of best efforts or good intentions, sometimes the reframe doesn't occur as effectively as we'd like. Here are some signs that it isn't working yet:

1. You're not getting introductions to prospective clients.
2. You feel alone in running the business.
3. You have a work group that reports individually to you, rather than a team invested in supporting one another through mutual accountability.
4. Clients and/or partners continue to frame you in the old way.
5. You aren't winning new clients.
6. Your assets aren't growing; your revenues aren't growing.
7. You feel like the business isn't fun anymore.
8. You are feeling burnt out.
9. There's turnover on your team.
10. Team members seem disengaged from the work and/or are unwilling to go the extra mile.

If you discover a preponderance of these signals or you otherwise have reason to believe that your reframe isn't working yet, set some time aside to investigate why. Have you worked all five steps of the reframing process? Have you put in sufficient time, teamwork, and resources when engaging in these steps? Are the services you offer out of alignment with what your ideal clients truly need? Have you failed to communicate your frame effectively?

An answer of yes to any of these questions could point you in the right direction for making adjustments. Use this book as a resource and/or consider working with a coach to further identify areas for improvement so you can get back on track and enjoy the many benefits of reframing yourself, your team, and your organization.

GO TO THE CLIENTWISE eXchange™

Along the journey of your reframe, you're going to test things out. You're going to make some new moves and you're going to try some new things, like a different message, different people, a different logo, or a different service model or approach. If you'd really like to be successful, you've got to get feedback from others; you have to test out whether your message is hitting the mark. We invite you to become a part of our community of reframers along the journey toward future success. We invite you to share your own reframes with us and with our community of advisors and leaders who are thinking about their own reframes and success.

When you find yourself in the midst of a reframe in the future, consider going to the eXchange™ to share your story just as advisors in this book have shared theirs. I believe that your own successes and challenges can offer useful lessons for others and, at ClientWise, we'd welcome hearing about it all on the eXchange™, which offers a platform for users to communicate with each other. You will find a specific group called "You've Been Framed," which you'll be able to join and participate in. We welcome you to learn more about the community and take advantage of what's been built here for you to learn alongside others who are also committed to growth and reframing as leaders. As you move through the reframe process, your team will learn and grow; your clients will share new ideas; you will deepen your own leadership skills. Those of us at ClientWise and in the ClientWise community would enjoy hearing about it and are willing to help you.

You never have to go it alone, then—not just because of the eXchange™ but because there are coaching and consulting companies like ClientWise that specialize in working with financial advisors and can partner with you to achieve any of the essential steps to reframing, from gathering client feedback and identifying ideal client type(s) to building the marketing assets needed to launch your new frame. What's more, you can bring coaching into your organization by training to earn the ClientWise Certified Financial Services Coach Designation, the only International Coach Federation (ICF)–approved course designed specifically to assist financial professionals in obtaining the vital skills needed to become an ICF-accredited coach. The options for support and community are waiting for you when you are ready.

KEY CONCEPT

You can find support for your reframe and help others by sharing what you've learned from your reframe by participating on the eXchange™.

CONCLUSION

No matter where you are in your business—no matter what your level of success—the most important thing is to consistently have an eye toward the future focused on how you, your team, and your firm want to be framed. Be willing to evolve, change, and grow as a journey learner.

Be curious about others, too. How can you help them achieve success? What do they find valuable in your existing partnership—both technical and relational aspects—and what would they love to have more of and less of from you and your firm in the future? Be curious about how others view you, your team, and your firm.

If we are to treat advising as a noble profession, then we must take the servant-leadership approach. This means becoming deeply connected to clients' needs as well as leading others on your team to connect deeply with clients. When we do our work well, we can truly shape the lives of others—those in our communities and in the world.

That being said, our industry is not without its challenges. We need to continue to raise the bar on fiduciary standards; we need to bring new talent into the industry; we need to find a way to not just help the ultra-affluent or the mass-affluent but also help every neighbor so that we can positively impact everyone's life. That may mean that your firm donates time to help those others.

We can feel good about the work that we do if we focus on the needs of our clients and also find a way to share the benefits of our work with everyone. It's time the public really understood the value of advice and the value you bring to helping shape a better

world. Get out there and frame yourselves, renew client relationships, and expand your reach, and you will help many others reach
their goals and live the lives they wish to lead. We can—and, I'm
confident, will—build a sustainable approach to the financial advising business.

Together, we can make this happen.

Additional Resources

Your purchase of *You've Been Framed* provides you with not only a comprehensive text but also access to online tools, available free on the ClientWise eXchange™ (youvebeenframed.clientwise.com), to assist you in your reframing journey. Each book-related tool on the eXchange™ is listed below for your convenience; more detailed descriptions of these tools can be found in each book chapter.

The truth is that I couldn't imagine writing this book without sharing these tools with you. Why? *You've Been Framed* is meant to be a starting point for your work and for a conversation that we in the industry can have with one another; the eXchange™ is a forum through which that work and conversation can continue. What's more, as the financial services profession and industry continue to evolve, the tools on the eXchange™ will be updated to keep things relevant, useful, and fresh.

The ClientWise eXchange™ is thus the container that allows this book to continue to evolve. No matter when you purchase the book or where you pick it up, so long as you're willing to take advantage of the many resources that exist online, they're yours. I invite you to join other financial leaders and your peers on the eXchange™ at youvebeenframed.clientwise.com so we can continue the conversation together!

Chapter 2
Online Tool 2.1: Your Wealth Management Checklist
　　A list highlighting key elements of each area of wealth management.

Chapter 3
Online Tool 3.1: Ten Reasons Your Clients Will Love You for Offering True Wealth Management
　　A list of 10 reasons your clients will love you for offering true wealth management that can be customized to your practice.

Chapter 4
Online Tool 4.1: Succession Planning Checklist
　　A checklist to use or adapt while planning your firm's leadership succession.

Chapter 5

Online Tool 5.1: Leader's Journey Assessment
> A 15-item assessment that will help you identify your current areas of strength as a team leader versus opportunities for growth.

Online Tool 5.2: A Guide to Defining Your High-Performing Team
> A 12-question guide to defining your unique high-performing team.

Chapter 6

Online Tool 6.1: Checklist for Conducting the ClientWise Conversation™ after a Client Review
> A how-to checklist on conducting the ClientWise Conversation™ successfully at the end of a client review, if a separate meeting is not possible.

Online Tool 6.2: ClientWise Conversation™ Data Collector
> A note-taking template to use during the ClientWise conversation to capture the client data.

Chapter 7

Online Tool 7.1: Example Needs, Target Market, Solutions, and Centers of Influence
> A template to help you define your new frame by thinking about the different target groups advisors can work with, along with their associated needs, solutions, and centers of influence.

Online Tool 7.2: Brainstorming the New Frame
> A step-by-step guide for defining your new frame, including a list of more than 70 power words and a variety of power phrases.

Chapter 8

Online Tool 8.1: A Guide to Defining Your High-Performing Team
> A 12-question guide to defining your unique high-performing team.

Online Tool 8.2: Ten Steps to Leading a Highly Effective Team
> A printable checklist of the 10 leadership behaviors you can engage in to become the most effective leader for your team.

Online Tool 8.3: Marketing Firms to Help You Build Your Brand
> A list of marketing firms that specialize in the financial services industry.

Online Tool 8.4: Marketing Campaign Organizer™
> An organizer that will help you outline your next marketing campaign, prompting thought about your target market, ideal client profile, possible offers, relevant messages, delivery options, who is involved, start and end dates, and expected ROI.

Chapter 9

Online Tool 9.1: Ninety-Nine Discovery Questions
> Ninety-nine discovery questions you can use to learn about the client.

Online Tool 9.2: Improve Your Client Acquisition Process
A printable copy of the Three Stages of the Client Acquisition Process™ and an associated exercise to help you improve your current process and set goals.

Chapter 10

Online Tool 10.1: The Advocate Approach Self-Assessment™
A tool to help you determine how engaged in the advocate approach you already are.
Online Tool 10.2: Potential Client Advocate Checklist
A checklist that will help you categorize clients into loyal advocates versus potential loyal advocates.
Online Tool 10.3: New Client Introduction Tracking Sheet
A tracking sheet that can be used to assess your introductions over the past 24 months and to record every new introduction.
Online Tool 10.4: Loyal Client Advocate Approach™ Key Findings Worksheet
A worksheet to help summarize key data you gathered during the ClientWise Conversation™.
Online Tool 10.5: Interview Questions for Potential Professional Advocates
A list of additional possible questions to ask potential professional advocates.

Conclusion

Online Tool C.1: A Checklist: Signals of Reframing Success
A downloadable checklist of signals that your reframe has been a success.

About the Author

Ray Sclafani is founder and CEO of ClientWise, the premier coaching and training company serving the financial services industry. Through ClientWise, Ray has provided coaching or created and presented workshops for, among others, Merrill Lynch, Morgan Stanley Wealth Management, UBS, LPL, Ameriprise Financial, Raymond James, MetLife, and Northwestern Mutual. In addition, he has spoken on request to major industry conferences and company events for firms such as Raymond James and FSC Securities, as well as the FPA National Conference, the John Hancock Funds Wholesaler Conference, the Nationwide Financial Summit Sales Conference, the MetLife Presidents' Conference, the Northwestern Mutual Forum, Northwestern Mutual's annual meeting, *Barron's* Winner's Circle Summit, and *Barron's* Top Advisory Teams Summit.

Prior to his leadership role at ClientWise, Ray served in the financial industry, where he worked at Alliance Bernstein for 20 years in several key roles, including founder and managing director of the Advisor Institute at Alliance Bernstein, where he developed and directed an extensive series of programs directed at creating sustainable motivation, increased sales, and deepened client relationships.

Through significant coaching education and practice, Ray earned the Professional Certified Coach (PCC) designation from the International Coach Federation, the leading independent professional association for coaches. He also holds a Master's Certification in Neuro-Linguistics from the International Association for Neuro-Linguistic Programming and has participated in The Strategic® Coach Program for 17 years. Ray holds a BA from Baylor University and lives in Bedford, New York, with his wife and true life partner, Beth, and their two sons, who continually inspire his work and his passion for excellence.

Index

Note: Page references in *italics* refer to figures.